VGM Opportunities Series

OPPORTUNITIES IN
MUSIC CAREERS

Robert Gerardi

Foreword by
Dr. Billy Taylor
Pianist, Composer, Recording
Artist, and Author

VGM Career Horizons
a division of *NTC Publishing Group*
Lincolnwood, Illinois USA

Cover Photo Credits:

Front cover: upper left, American Conservatory of Music; upper right, photo by Jack Van Antwerp, courtesy of The Cleveland Orchestra; lower left, Wayne and Mary Brill, Interlochen photo; lower right, Old Town School of Folk Music.

Back cover: upper left, Wayne and Mary Brill, Interlochen photo; upper right, American Music Conference; lower left, Bob Gerardi; lower right, The Curtis Institute of Music.

Library of Congress Cataloging-in-Publication Data

Gerardi, Robert.
    Opportunities in music careers/Robert Gerardi.—2nd ed.

        p. cm.—(VGM opportunities series)
    Includes bibliographical references.
    ISBN 0–8442–8154–9: $12.95.—ISBN 0–8442–8155–7 (pbk.): $9.95
    1. Music—Vocational guidance. I. Title. II. Series.
ML3795.G47 1991
780'.23'73—dc20
                                         90–50739
                                             CIP
                                           MN

ABOUT THE AUTHOR

Bob Gerardi has been a professional entertainer for more than 30 years. His credits include working as a recording artist, nightclub singer, studio singer, pianist, band leader, music director, composer, producer, songwriter, voice teacher, author, and actor. Mr. Gerardi has performed on radio, television, and in film; in nightclubs, hotels, restaurants, cocktail lounges, and theaters; in concert and in recording studios.

A native New Yorker who was born in Brooklyn, Gerardi now resides in New York City's Upper West Side. He began studying classical piano at the age of six and learned to play guitar in his early teens, singing and playing country and popular songs in school and at parties.

Mr. Gerardi began his professional music career as a teenager in the late fifties, when his rock-and-roll band was the first to be introduced into the club date circuit by society orchestra leader, Lester Lanin. The band also hit the Top 10 with two of their songs. Bob wrote one of the songs, which still gets airplay on New York's WCBS/FM. The station also sponsors Don K. Reed's "Doo Whap Shop," where Mr. Gerardi is a frequent guest, discussing his career in music and fifties trivia.

Mr. Gerardi graduated from the American Academy of Dramatic Arts, attended Manhattan School of Music, NYU Film School, and the School of Visual Arts. He studied voice with Richard Field and coached with William Spada, studied composition with Hall Overton, the Shillinger system of composition with Richard Benda, and jazz piano with Don Friedman.

Presently Mr. Gerardi composes and produces original music for feature film, television, and commercials; he sings and plays the piano in New York City's hotel circuit and teaches voice, as well as performing as an actor in numerous television commercials.

He is presently serving on the Board of Governors of the New York Friars Club.

ACKNOWLEDGMENTS

I would like to thank the following individuals and organizations for their help in making this book possible.

Second Edition

Jacalyn Alexa Davis, editor/assistant; Jack L. Green, agent/entrepreneur; James DiPasquale, film composer; John Francis, Central Opera Service; Dr. Andrea Farbman, National Association of Music Therapy; Martha Perry, Opera America; Richard Whelan, National Council for Education Statistics; Dr. George Butler, CBS Records; Johnny Bienstock, TRF Production Music Library; Frank Military, Sr. V.P., Warner/Chappell Music Inc; Don Friedman, jazz pianist/teacher; Cantor Bernard Beer, Yesheva University, New York; Errol Dante, nightclub singer/actor; John Mahoney, staff producer/Synclavier programmer, Atlantic Records; Victoria J. O'Reilly, American Symphony Orchestra League; Wendy Goldstein-Ishkhans, Sr. Dir. A&R, RCA Records; Chuck Walker, Muzak Inc.; Sherry Eaker, Backstage Publications; Eugene Holly, National Jazz Service Organization; Virginia Falck, National Endowment for the Arts; Cathy Bennett, New Music Seminar; Joey Rapp, Conference of Personal Managers.

First Edition

Els Sincebaugh; John Hart; LeBaron Taylor, CBS Records; Dr. George Butler, CBS Records; Maggie Cavender, Nashville Songwriters Association Intl.; Robert McCrillis, Columbia Artists Corp.; Robin McCabe; Bert Lucarelli; Gordon Harrell; the late Irwin Schuster, Chappell Music; Jean Thomas Fox, Kids & Co.; Mary Seldon Cramer, Shaw Artists Corp.; Manhattan School of Music, N.Y.C.; Tim Ledwith, Allegro; Lew Waldeck, American Federation of Musicians; American Federation of Television & Radio Artists; Belmont College, Nashville; George David Weiss, AGAC/The Songwriters Guild; Antony Payne, Bob Giraldi Prods.; Dorothy Spears, Dick Moore & Assoc.; Matthew Cvetic; Rosemary Leeder; Ed Noward, National Association of Music Therapy; George Butcher; Charlie Birch; Annemarie Woletz Franco, International Musician; Nancy Clarck, American Music Center; Lt. Commander Ascione, United States Navy; Major Sheip, United States Army; Major Day, United States Marine Corps; United States Air Force; the late William Spada; Melanie Jarratt, American Symphony Orchestra League; Central Opera Service; Harold Horowitz, National Endowment for the Arts; Sylvia Dunsky, United Federation of Teachers; Ellen Blassingham, Opera America; Lucy Battersby, Metropolitan National Council; Tom Snyder, National Center for Education Statistics; Gary Chicofsky; Tony Lupo; Harold Rifkin.

FOREWORD

The music field is an exciting mosaic of unique opportunities. There is a need for innovative, creative, and knowledgeable people in every phase of the business side of this art form.

Most people are attracted to the glamorous and highly visible performance side of the music field, but for a variety of reasons, they end up in management, production, recording, publishing, music education, or other fields in which their musical education and experience can give them an edge.

I am a working musician and, like many of my colleagues, I require a large group of professionals to help me achieve my career goals. I have a management team that books my engagements, a public relations firm that promotes all my various activities, a music business lawyer who advises me on the many legal issues and contracts that govern almost all my activities, an accountant who helps me keep track of the money I owe, and the money owed to me. A record company and a publishing company publish and promote my music, and an investment counselor advises me on nonmusical investments I make.

This support system gives me a great deal of control over my creative output and enables me to add television, radio, and educational projects to my already crowded schedule, in ways which maximize the use of my time, knowledge, and experience.

Nearly everyone on my support team is a musician or has some background experience in music, and the insights they have developed make them more effective in helping me solve career related problems. They are resourceful and indispensable to me.

If you are interested and attracted to the broad and diversified field of music, look beyond the performance area and examine the legal, technical, educational, and financial aspects of the apparatus that supports that area.

You may find that you are uniquely qualified to contribute to the field and to your own personal development by establishing your presence as an important contributor in that part of the music field which enables you to capitalize on your strengths, training, and experience.

Reading this book is a very good start.

> Dr. Billy Taylor
> Pianist, Composer, Recording
> Artist, and Author

PREFACE

You're sitting in a dental office or dining in an elegant restaurant, and the sound of music fills the air. It's with you in the elevator, in your car, on your train or plane trip. You can take music home and play it on your stereo, hear it on television, or carry it with you in a Walkman.

Music can inspire national pride, young love, and high spirits. It can make you remember, make you forget, or just make you feel good. Music can make you dance, sing, or put you to sleep. It sells hamburgers, toothpaste, and soft drinks; it tells you where to vacation and how to get there.

Try to imagine a movie without music, or a day without music, or a world without music . . . impossible. Music is the universal language that touches us all. Its trends may change; artists and songs may come and go, but music has been, and always will be, a part of our lives.

The music business today is a multibillion dollar industry, involving many fascinating and exciting careers, especially for the few who achieve stardom. Performers who achieve star status are like huge corporations, and like any other corporation, they require the behind-the-scenes talents of a large variety of people to function.

Years ago, Big Bands employed many musicians to create their sound, but traveling was difficult, record sales were small (compared to today), media coverage was limited, and a string of one-night stands performing to small audiences generally didn't bring in large profits.

Today the bands are smaller, and their sound is electronic. Amplification makes it possible to play to large audiences. Modern transportation can zip groups from one concert to another, and it takes a host of people to put that show on the road. Concerts are broadcast live, and also videotaped and transmitted at a later date via satellite systems all around the world, making it possible to play to an audience of millions. As the artist's popularity increases, record sales go into the millions, and the modern one-night stand can reap huge amounts of revenue. It's a big business with many career opportunities.

The popular recording artist enjoys the most lucrative side of the business, and the musician/singer/songwriter with star status is at the top of the field. Popular music is the most competitive area of music, but as difficult as it may seem to break into, the industry continues to need new and creative talent with fresh ideas.

Beyond the glamour of popular music stardom, however, vast numbers of other performing and nonperforming careers exist at all levels and in all varieties of music. For example, in hotels, resorts, restaurants and clubs, thousands of musicians and singers are employed—from a single pianist to strolling violins, from a small combo to a large orchestra. Wherever there's entertainment, you'll find working professional musicians.

Take a look at the roster of artists classified as stars, and try to imagine the network of careers behind each one. For example, a single star performer needs back-up musicians, back-up singers, arrangers, writers, an accompanist, a copyist, conductors, engineers, sound and lighting people, agents, managers, public relations people, and wardrobe, hair, and makeup people. A great number of jobs exist in record companies, publishing companies, advertising agencies, and recording studios, as well as in radio, television, and film. All these businesses need beginners as well as seasoned professionals.

All of the different forms of music provide opportunities for musicians, singers, and composers. There are jobs for those who love opera, classical music, musical theater, jazz, country, pop, rock, and gospel.

Every city in the United States and Canada wants a part of the cultural scene. Many cities now have their own opera houses, ballet companies, symphony orchestras, musical theaters, concert halls, and convention centers. Each of these provides additional opportunities in music.

American music is more creative and inventive today than ever before, influenced by the classics, the golden age of the American composer, the Big Bands, jazz, the fifties, rock, rhythm and blues, country, and newer trends. As new technologies and new forms of music continue to emerge, so will more new and exciting opportunities.

Making music is a business, and as in any other business, you need talent, training, and experience along with confidence, personality, and determination. Most important of all, you must have a strong desire to succeed; you must want success enough to be willing to overcome all obstacles. Some of the most successful businesspeople in America started at the bottom and worked their way up through many failures and setbacks to make it to the top of their profession. It takes courage and hard work.

Many people approach the music business tentatively, waiting for someone to do it for them. That's not how it works. If you are ambitious and creative, there's a job waiting for you, but you have to find it, and get it, for yourself.

As in any profession, when you're starting at square one, you must have a plan. That plan should be a step-by-step strategy to become a working professional, to earn a living in the music business, working with and for your peers. Your first job leads to your second, your second to your third, and so on. This process requires a keen understanding of where your talents lie; it involves understanding the needs of the business and learning how and where to find work.

Musicians and singers love their work, and no work is more satisfying than a labor of love. Many musicians are multitalented, playing several instruments, singing, acting, composing, teaching, and arranging. They find many ways to create jobs and survive while working toward that "big break." More often than not, that big break never comes. Many musicians work hard at finding work all their lives, and even short periods of job security are rare. Nevertheless, there are some relatively steady jobs in music, and the industry has grown larger in recent years. So, if you are interested in becoming a working professional in the music world, you will need good information to get started and to continue to compete successfully for jobs.

In writing this book, I had the opportunity to meet many interesting and successful people. I made some new friends, and renewed some old friendships. I was able to look back on my own career and draw from my mistakes and successes.

I remember a point in my career when I wanted to work in publishing. One of the largest music publishing companies was looking for a professional manager to run the New York office. I wanted the job very badly.

A friend of mine knew the head of the company and introduced us over the phone. An appointment was set, and we met at the Essex House and had a pleasant conversation. We discussed many things, but I was not offered the job. I left the meeting confused, and it took me a long time to understand why I didn't get the offer. I went to that meeting solely as a musician. I was a singer, a pianist, and a songwriter, but he already knew that. What he was looking for was a corporate executive, a businessperson.

The lesson is this: had I been prepared with some business and management studies or experience, I would have had something extra to add to that conversation, and I might have gotten that job.

Today, the music business is becoming more and more complex and competitive, and you've got to meet the challenge.

Whether you're university-trained or the street-fighter brand of musician, you still need experience, and there's only one way to get it: through hard work and preparation. It means trying again and again for that job, working and learning more, and going back again. It's a challenging and rewarding field if you're ambitious, talented, and creative, but you've got to take command and plan your own destiny.

In music, one thing is certain: you will get out of your work what you put into it. Good luck.

CONTENTS

CHAPTER 1

GETTING STARTED

You just performed at a friend's party, or sang at a local club, and everyone is congratulating you on how good you sound. In fact, someone even says, "What are you doing here? You should be in the big time! You sound as good as the people I've heard on television."

For the first time, you realize that all the years of practice and study have paid off, and you know yourself that you sound as good as some of the professionals. Not only that, but you really enjoy performing. So you make your decision and announce to an unenthusiastic family, "I'm going to become a professional musician." You go to New York or Hollywood, and in two weeks, there you are: a star with your own TV show.

Unfortunately, it's not that easy. If it were, there would be 250 million people with their own TV shows. Everyone would be in the music business. Many people fantasize about conducting Beethoven's Fifth Symphony, singing like Frank Sinatra, Barbara Mandrel, Michael Jackson, Paula Abdul, or another superstar.

Most people see only the tip of the iceberg. They see nothing of the reality behind the fantasy: a network of exciting and lucrative careers that seldom get attention. Dreams of being in the music business are not bad, but it takes hard work and talent to

1

make them come true. A dream without a plan remains a dream. To think that you can step into the spotlight without the necessary training and experience is to give in to delusions of grandeur.

Those who think it is easy to succeed in the music business are in for a big shock. But it would also be unfair to assume that it is impossible to make it. Examine the many diverse careers in music; be aware of the opportunities available as a professional musician. There's much more to the music business than just the bright lights.

Someone has to design and build the musical instruments, tune and repair them, and teach people to play them. The music itself has to be created, arranged and scored, copied and transcribed, and then printed as sheet music. It is then published and sold to the public. In order to record the music, musicians, a producer, an engineer, and a recording studio staff must work together to convert the sound into a record. Each record company has a large marketing staff to distribute recordings to broadcasters and retail stores. Large organizations monitor the sale and performance of the music. Many musicians play music live: a pianist at a house party, a small combo in a cocktail lounge, a dance band, or a large symphony orchestra.

The music business consists of so many levels—from artistic creation to assembly line production; from spotlight glitter to matter-of-fact business; from managers, lawyers, agents, technicians, and an entire cast of supporting players to a simple country picker singing about a train.

DO YOU HAVE WHAT IT TAKES?

Talent alone is not the key to success in the music business. It takes an aggressive (not to be confused with obnoxious) person to seize important opportunities. And every time you do, you risk rejection. Do you have the courage to stand up and try again? An artist has to have strength and optimism in order to survive.

Rejection can be painful and frustrating. If you let it soak in and take it personally, it can destroy you as an artist and as a person. Do you have the confidence to know where your talents lie and the conviction to "go for it"? Do you have the humility to know where your weaknesses are and the intelligence to study and work at improving yourself? It's not easy.

Thomas Edison failed thousands of times before he succeeded in inventing the light bulb. Are you willing to go the extra distance for your success? Do you have the discipline to practice endless hours and study constantly, knowing that you will slide backwards if you falter? Can you tolerate the auditions, the loneliness, the travel, the living away from home, friends, and family? Are you willing to give up your weekends, evenings, and vacations in order to succeed? Are you ready to accept the fact that even though you're an artist, you must become a businessperson as well?

Show business is filled with stories of superstars who were told that they didn't have it, to go home and give it up. Yet they persisted, and we admire those very people for their professional achievements.

CAREER GOALS AND PLANS

Over a thousand colleges, universities, conservatories, and specialty schools teach music and music related subjects. Thousands of students major in composition and instrumental or vocal performance, not to mention those studying music education, music therapy, and music business. Add to that students who study privately, and those who are self-taught, and the number of prospective professional musicians is mind-boggling. Each one has the same aspiration: to get a job and make it to the top in an already overcrowded industry.

How do you break into the world of music, overcoming the fierce competition and the overwhelming odds? Not everyone can. Success needs to be measured not by stardom, but by the ability to make a living at your chosen profession. Simply surviving in the music business is success in itself.

Getting started in music is no different than any other business. You have to become a working professional and work your way up. Most beginners, although excellent musicians, are not self-motivated. They tend to think that someone will discover them. Waiting to be discovered is pointless; you have to get up and do it yourself. Gordon Harrell (Broadway conductor and arranger), Robin McCabe (concert pianist and recording artist), and Bert Lucarelli (concert oboist and recording artist) all respond similarly to the question, ''How did you make it to where you are?'' They explain that they knew exactly what they wanted, they went after it, and everything fell into place. You have to know what you want in order to get it.

First off, develop clear goals. Once you know exactly what you want to do, then you can develop a plan. The plan can consist of learning a repertoire to win a competition or getting a job that will give you the necessary experience, credit and exposure to move on to your next job. You may need a plan just to survive until something better comes along.

There are two types of people who try to make it in the music business: those who want overnight success and those who are willing to build their careers more slowly. The first group is usually chasing a show business dream with lots of good intentions and wishful thinking. And they usually fall by the wayside with clichés like, ''It's not what you know, but who you know'' or ''I never get the breaks.'' Those who seek overnight success want the glamour right away, but they don't understand the hard work required.

Other aspiring musicians build their careers more slowly. They are architects of success, learning how the music business works, discovering what opportunities are available, where to find them, and how to get them. These musicians survive on the lesser jobs, while keeping tuned in to the better ones; they build a network of connections, working as a professional, with professionals, and meeting the right people.

The opportunities in music are so diverse that it is an injustice to have only one objective in mind. You should be willing to step into another music related career that can keep you in the business. So, begin forming your plan of attack, but make it a flexible, realistic one. Build your career carefully, and you will enjoy a long and successful life in the music industry.

PREPARATION

You should start your career when you feel you are ready. Your teachers can help you with that decision, but if you're not ready for the professional world, you will be the first to know. Preparing for a career in music takes years of lessons, practicing, and building a repertoire, and it never ends. If you think the preparation is only difficult in the beginning stages of your career, then you are in for a surprise. Once you become a professional, the preparation not only continues, but intensifies. As you develop your career, the competition becomes keener, and you must stay in top shape to meet it. The preparation is both behind you and ahead of you.

You should meet the challenge with curiosity and openness. The more you know, the more you will have to draw on. Be aware of the many different musical styles, look into other areas of the arts, such as painting, sculpture, dance, acting, and poetry. Learn the technical and the business aspects of music. Most musicians and singers are multitalented. Develop a variety of skills; besides making you a better performer, these skills may also help you survive.

SURVIVAL

Everyone faces good times and bad times in life, but musicians tend to get more than their share of the bad times. At a very early point in your career, you should develop a strong will to survive. Survival sometimes means having to take a couple of steps back before going forward again. During lean periods you may find yourself working in some real dives for little money and little applause, but you can learn a great deal from this experience, continue paying your rent, and be wiser and stronger when a better job comes along. Many of today's concert artists and conductors survived as section players in orchestras until their break came along. Even today's popular singers and musicians survived playing club dates and saloons.

Good Habits

Mr. August Ceradini, who was manager of the St. Regis–Sheraton Hotel in New York City, looks for these characteristics in a musician: punctuality, neat appearance, pleasant personality, no bad habits, and ability to do the job. Any club owner, agent, or band leader would say the same thing. Would you hire a person who was insecure, unhappy, and negative? Would you want to work with a person who was uncooperative, lazy, late for work, and sloppy in appearance?

Good habits will help you build a good reputation and a network of return engagements. Good habits are key to survival in the music business. In the business, creative, and performance end of music, it still takes dependable, conscientious people to get a job done.

Marketing

Knowing where you fit in should be obvious. Do you love classical or jazz, country or rock? Do you enjoy solo work, playing with an ensemble, or do you want to be the leader? Do you prefer studio work, public performance, or composing? Knowing what you want to do will guide your career and drive you towards your long-term goal. Still, you need to survive along the way.

Adjusting your talents for different markets is one way of getting the bread-and-butter work. Learn the style and repertoire to play a cocktail lounge, a club date, or a restaurant. Learn some additional skills in order to work in a record or publishing company. Move to an area that has more opportunities available to you. All of these skills can be part of your survival strategy.

PROMOTION

Promoting yourself means making your talents known. Even the biggest stars need constant promotion to keep both the industry and the public aware of them. A record album, a concert, a television special, or a movie all require promotion in order to succeed. Established entertainers pay large sums of money to press agents and public relations firms to keep their names in the public eye.

As the laws of physics state, for every action there is a reaction. The action of promoting çauses the reaction of interest. Cause enough interest, and opportunities will begin to open up to you.

You might have all the talent in the world, but unless you tell someone about it, you're just singing in the shower. The technique of self-promotion involves having a bag of tricks, or tools with which to make friends and attract attention.

The Inside Tools

The inside tools for getting started are confidence, personality, and a positive attitude. Don't underestimate the importance of that statement. If you are a happy person and love music, it will show. If you don't love music, you're in the wrong business.

You will also need a good sense of humor. In order to survive the pressures of the music business, you'll have to know how to laugh at it, and sometimes at yourself. Another important tool is supportive friends, relatives, associates, and teachers. It is hard to develop a career in music when surrounded by negativity, doubt, fear, and superstition.

The Outside Tools

In addition to the right attitude and personality, an aspiring musician needs some basic business tools to launch a career. These include business cards, stationery, resume, photographs, flyers, postcards, press kit, demos, and an answering machine or service. Once you have these basic tools of self-promotion, you will need to use them in combination with a system of networking, auditioning, and making the rounds to look for jobs. Some young performers look for places to showcase their talent or set up debut recitals. These are the outside tools for starting your career in music.

BUSINESS CARDS

A business card should be simple, elegant, and straightforward. It should list your name, your talent, and a telephone number where you can be reached. An address is optional. Since this card is to represent you, it should be the highest quality you can afford. It might be wise to consider artwork, a logo, color, or special type, so that your card will stand out from your competitors'.

THE TELEPHONE

The telephone is probably the most important instrument you'll ever use. It has the power to open doors, and lets you introduce yourself and make appointments. You can talk to an agent or a producer in Los Angeles, New York, or anywhere in the world.

Before you start to run up an expensive printing bill for business cards, be sure you have a permanent phone number. Some people like to have an answering service and use that number on their cards. That way, each time you change your address and phone number, your stationery won't be affected. It is very unprofessional to have a phone that doesn't answer, or one that's answered by a kid sister, a grandfather, or a roommate, groping for a pencil. If you live with other people, get a separate business phone number and have a pickup service or an automatic phone answering machine.

THE RESUME

Your resume should be well planned and carefully laid out. The reader should be able to use it as a road map of your career.

First and foremost, give your name, address, telephone and social security numbers, and your affiliation with any professional organizations (such as unions or guilds). Membership in these organizations establishes you immediately as a working professional. Next, indicate your main talent, your instrument (violin, trumpet, piano), or voice and range.

Then list the most important and impressive credits first, starting with the most recent and working backward. Also indicate any competitions, awards, or scholarships you have won, and describe your training—formal and private. Finally, mention any notable special abilities such as second instruments, composing, arranging, copying, or transcribing.

The resume should be neat, easy-to-read, and honest. Don't fill it with items that waste the reader's time. Above all, be truthful. One false statement and the validity of your whole resume is threatened.

Since most musicians and singers are multitalented, you may need several versions of your resume, each emphasizing a different specialty. Perhaps you're a singer whose main objective is opera, but you also make a living singing religious music; then you should have two resumes. One resume would present the religious credits and repertoire first, and the other would stress the opera career.

NTC Publishing Group, 4255 W. Touhy, Lincolnwood, IL 60646-1975 publishes *How to Write a Winning Resume,* a book that explains how to put together a resume and compose a cover letter. Also, the Superintendent of Documents makes a catalog available that lists the pamphlet *Resumes, Application Forms, Cover Letters, and Interviews.* The pamphlet explains how to prepare a resume, write a letter of application, and have a successful interview. The pamphlet costs one dollar, and the catalog is available for free by writing to the Consumer Information Center, Pueblo, CO 81002.

If you can afford it, consider using a good quality paper when having your resume reproduced. Stationery is also something to consider. It is professional to have cover letters and envelopes imprinted with a letterhead on quality paper. If your budget will allow, a little flash won't hurt.

PHOTOGRAPHS

Photographs are another important tool for promoting yourself. Your 8-by-10-inch glossy should be taken by a professional photographer and should be a good likeness of yourself. It should convey warmth and personality, so that whoever looks at it will want to meet you or, better yet, hire you. You may also want to have some photos of yourself in performance.

FLYERS

A flyer is an advertisement that can be mailed to anyone you feel is important to your career. It should contain your name; the place, time, and date of your engagement; and your picture. Depending upon your budget, it can be simply typed and duplicated on a copy machine, or it can incorporate some artwork, have typeset text, and be prepared by a printer.

POSTCARDS

Postcards, preferably with your picture on one side, can be very effective. Use them as a flyer or as a follow-up to a flyer or performance. A postcard is a sure way of getting your face, name, and message onto someone's desk. Think of yourself as a product that has to be packaged and advertised. Repetition and persistence are needed to sell a product.

PRESS KIT

Think of a press kit (or portfolio) as a do-it-yourself-kit. It's a package of all the publicity from past performances. A press kit can be a collage of newspaper clippings, advertisements, reviews, write-ups, flyers, and programs. As in the resume, the most impressive and most recent credits should be up front.

The press kit should be entertaining and informative and should be more than just a bunch of xerox copies stapled together. It takes careful planning and a good eye to create an interesting layout and presentation.

In order to build a press kit, you need to have something to put in it. Try to get some form of coverage for each engagement. Inviting the local press, making sure that each booking is advertised in the local newspaper, and sending out flyers are all effective forms of promotion.

Your press kit can be presented in a plastic or paper folder, the type that can be purchased in any good stationery store. If your budget allows, the kit can be bound with your name imprinted on the cover.

DEMO

The demo, short for demonstration record, is a good way to audition, especially for a job that's far from your home. There are two types of demos: audio and video. Most people prefer to use a cassette audiotape since it's easier to handle. The demo, like the resume and press kit, should be well planned. It should be short, entertaining, and include a variety of your best performances. A demo can be recorded at home, at a live performance, or in a studio. Although it is more expensive to do a demo in a professional recording studio, the difference may be worth it. The more professional the recording, the better you will sound.

The video cassette is also becoming a popular means of auditioning talent. There are two types of video demos: the VHS and the 3/4-inch professional cassette. Many agents and producers prefer the VHS, which allows them to view performers at their own convenience in the comfort and privacy of their offices or homes.

NETWORKING

Networking means meeting the right people. The best way to get to know other musicians, singers, and writers is through professional organizations. Unions, guilds, and associations all have members with a shared interest in music. Attend meetings, seminars, and workshops; get involved in their activities and special projects, all of which will afford you the opportunity to meet people in the music business.

Showcase clubs are another good place to meet people. If you have talent and an open personality, it shouldn't be hard to make friends. The trade papers, or a local entertainment directory, should have a list of showcase clubs. The yellow pages list record companies, publishing companies, and agents. Making the rounds and meeting people is the best way to build connections.

Every audition or job gives you a chance to meet people who can give you advice and help in building your career. Doing a good job will help you get recommended for other work. And, in turn, you can recommend other people for jobs. It's all a matter of getting into the inner circle and building a reputation and a good relationship with other working professionals.

ROUNDS

When an artist makes rounds, he or she is like a salesperson going from door to door with a product. The artist faces the same challenge, and the same possible rejection, as any other salesperson. However, since the artist is both the salesperson and the product, he or she must do all the work alone.

First of all, a campaign strategy must be planned out. Start with a list of names, addresses, and phone numbers of anyone you think you need to know: agents, managers, record company executives, publishers, and club owners. Make phone calls to introduce yourself and make appointments. Develop a good phone technique, and keep accurate records of each call. If they ask you to call back in three days, or tell you not to call again, you need to follow up the conversation appropriately.

Learn how to be persistent without being a pest. A phone call can be followed by a mailing, a picture and resume, a follow-up letter, a flyer, or a postcard. Managers, agents, and executives are very busy people and don't generally see anyone without an appointment. However, they do have good memories and will remember your name and recognize the fact that you were knocking on their door. Eventually, your persistence will be noticed.

AUDITIONS

An audition is a job application, and you must demonstrate your talent. In most cases, there isn't enough time to give an extensive example of your work, so you must plan carefully to select material that shows your best qualities in a very short time.

Many singers and musicians get overly ambitious and try to tackle material that's not right for them. This is a mistake. Even superstars have to audition for a movie or a Broadway play, and the audition material must be suited to both the performer and the particular audition.

A career in music is also a career in job hunting; learning how to audition and how to enjoy auditioning is a giant step in the right direction. It's important to have a good attitude, a good personality, confidence, and to love what you are doing. All of this will show at the audition.

Not getting the job does not mean your performance was bad. In most cases it simply means they were looking for a different type of performer. It's important to come away from the audition happy and satisfied that you did a good job. The way you feel about yourself and your work has a great effect on the quality of future performances; therefore, you must have a positive attitude. A string of good auditions is guaranteed to get you a job sooner or later.

SHOWCASES

In the early days of vaudeville, the audience booed, hissed, and threw vegetables at the entertainer if they didn't like the act. Someone backstage would administer the final blow by dragging the entertainer off the stage with a big hook.

Today, the showcase stage is tough, like the stages of vaudeville. And even though we're too civilized for vegetables and hooks, the audience still determines each performer's fate. Every performance is a showcase, and the next project and connection depend on the previous performance. For example, you may be working in one club and invite the owner of another club to sample your work for possible future engagements.

The showcase is a much misunderstood concept. In recent years it has come to mean free music, and many club owners have taken advantage of young talent in need of a place to perform. These clubs serve expensive drinks while the acts work for little or no pay. The audience consists of people the performers invited themselves, by using their own money to print and mail out flyers advertising the performance. Still, this format is an important part of beginning a career in music. A singer or musician can use a showcase to her or his advantage. A showcase allows performers to break in an act; try out new material in front of a live audience; and invite agents, club owners, managers, and the press.

Many entertainers get caught up in the showcase syndrome and end up doing it just for the applause. At the same time, many entertainers have been discovered in showcase clubs and have moved on to become celebrities, or at least have gained the experience necessary to become working professionals.

RECITALS

Many soloists come to New York to get national recognition as a concert artist. After a period of free-lancing, knocking on doors, and auditioning, they may decide to present themselves in a debut recital. It's a risky and expensive proposition, but some have made it work to their advantage.

To give a recital, you have to rent a hall, advertise, give every friend and relative a ticket, and invite arts managers who generally don't like to attend these kinds of recitals. If you are studying with a well-respected teacher whose word is highly regarded, the managers may show up.

Reviewers are the most important people to invite since a favorable press review can gain the interest of the arts managers. An unfavorable review may cause some people to run from the business. Others just study more, practice harder, continue working, and try it all over again.

CHAPTER 2

THE SERIOUS PERFORMER

ORCHESTRAS

According to the American Symphony Orchestra League, there are over 1,600 symphony orchestras in this country that employ full-time, part-time, and student musicians. Symphony orchestras can be divided into three categories: (1) orchestras with expenses over $1 million, (2) orchestras with expenses between $260,000 and $1 million, and (3) orchestras with expenses less than $260,000. There are 103 orchestras in the first category, 101 in the second, and 1,030 orchestras in the third category. The 40 largest orchestras collectively employed 3,525 musicians in the 1988–89 season. Large orchestras employ 85 to 105 players, while smaller ones employ 60 to 75 players. Some players are paid on a contract basis with a yearly salary, vacation, and benefits, while others are hired on a per-performance basis.

Rehearsal and performance schedules can be very demanding. For example, in the 1988–89 season, the New York Philharmonic reported 199 performances; the Boston Symphony Orchestra, 251; the Chicago Symphony Orchestra, 185; the Philadelphia Symphony Orchestra, 186; the Pittsburgh Symphony Orchestra, 166;

17

the Cincinnati Symphony Orchestra, 147; the Cleveland Symphony Orchestra, 181; the Los Angeles Philharmonic, 194; the San Francisco Symphony Orchestra, 195; the Detroit Symphony Orchestra, 165; and the Minnesota Symphony Orchestra, 195. A season runs from 29 to 52 weeks, with 24 orchestras guaranteeing a 52-week season.

Salaries range from $140 to $1,200 per week; however, yearly salaries in orchestras with budgets over $1 million range from $14,000 to $57,000. Musicians who work a short season have to find ways of supplementing their incomes. Those who work on a per-performance basis usually receive a prorated salary. A wage scale chart is available from the American Federation of Musicians, 1501 Broadway, New York, NY 10036.

Most orchestras prefer the standard works of classical composers. Therefore, a musician should be familiar with the standard repertoire. There are, however, some orchestras that specialize in performing twentieth-century compositions.

Orchestral Training

Musicianship among orchestra members is of the highest caliber, and ability to read music is essential. Being able to work well with a large group and to follow directions is very important. A musician generally starts studying at a very early age, and after many years of private instruction, he or she should also study at a university or conservatory. Studying with a performer in a major symphony can be very important to a younger musician's career.

Constant ensemble work and experience are necessary to qualify for a symphony orchestra. There are many college orchestras to train with, as well as summer workshops. Teachers and schools often have information that can help you find these workshops and positions with orchestras.

The National Federation of Music Clubs publishes a guide to scholarships and awards. It lists categories and requirements for scholarships from the various colleges and universities that offer summer workshops.

Finding Jobs

Openings for musicians in symphony orchestras can be found in the back of *International Musician,* the official journal of the American Federation of Musicians. The July 1990 issue advertised 176 openings for various instruments in 50 different orchestras. *International Musician* also lists ads for scholarships, fellowships, competitions, and seminars. You should consider subscribing to the journal. For information, write to *International Musician,* 1501 Broadway, New York, NY 10036.

The American Symphony Orchestra League has available to its members their publication, *Symphony Magazine,* and also three job bulletins: *Administrative Service Announcements* (bimonthly), *Conducting Service Announcements* (monthly), and *Musicians Service Announcements* (monthly). The league now offers a new service to its members: a resume clearinghouse that lists members for future referrals.

If you are considering moving to another part of the country, you should also read the local union newsletter.

Openings are often found by word of mouth; therefore, being in the orchestra system is the best way of finding work.

To apply for a position, you must send a resume and, in some cases, a tape. If the audition is far away from your home, you may have to pay for your own travel expenses. Auditions are held behind a screen, so that no prejudices will enter into the judgment.

Supplemental Work

Most musicians who work in major symphony, opera, or ballet orchestras spend their entire careers in one position. That makes for a very tight job market. Sometimes up to 90 hopefuls will apply for a position. Many symphony musicians also play in smaller chamber orchestras, which also advertise openings in *International Musician.* Chamber Music America, 545 Eighth Avenue, New York, NY 10018 is another good source of leads. They publish a quarterly magazine, *Chamber Music;* a membership directory; and *The Directory of Summer Chamber Music Workshops. Musical America Directory of the Performing Arts* has a complete listing of symphony and chamber orchestras. *High Fidelity/Musical America,* a monthly magazine, contains symphony, opera, and concert news.

Many symphonic musicians perform in solo recitals or in duos, trios, quartets, and ensembles. Many private affairs and restaurants will hire a classical string quartet or a harpist, sometimes alternating with a dance band. Check with local contractors and club date bandleaders who book music for private affairs.

In one year in the United States, six thousand students graduated with degrees in performance. In that same year, there were about 400 openings in symphony orchestras. A young musician generally has to become part of the free-lance pool to earn a living and has to frequently audition while waiting for a break. It often takes from three to five years of near poverty for a young musician to get that break. And there are no guarantees. Luck, timing, and politics all play important parts in establishing yourself.

Positions Available

In addition to the actual players, each orchestra offers many behind-the-scenes positions that need to be filled: general manager, assistant manager, public relations director, fundraising coordinator. There are jobs for musicians as well, such as librarian or stage manager. If you are studying with a symphony musician, you might try to work at one of those jobs until a back chair is open. A knowledge of business and management might be an asset. For most of these jobs, you may have to be a member of the American Federation of Musicians.

INSTRUMENTS

These are the instruments of the orchestra:

- *Strings:* violin, viola, cello, double bass.
- *Woodwinds:* piccolo, flute, bass flute, oboe, English horn, small clarinet, bass clarinet, bassoon, double bassoon.
- *Horns:* cornet, trumpet, French horn, trombone, tuba.
- *Percussion:* piano, kettle drums, celesta, glockenspiel, xylophone, bells, triangle, tambourine, snare, bass drum, cymbals, gong, and others.

The ability to play other instruments related to your main instrument can be a valuable asset in getting work with orchestras. Also, playing in studios and musical theater requires the ability to double; that is, to play more than one instrument. In fact, some musicians have switched instruments several times before finding their niche.

SOLO CONCERT PERFORMERS

The career of a concert artist begins at a very early age. Studying with a highly qualified teacher who can recognize and develop the qualities of virtuosity, and guide your career, is essential. Although a young musician may have studied privately for many years developing technique and repertoire, a university or conservatory education still is extremely important. The high level of training, the energy of the school environment, and the constant exposure to other equally talented students will provide the fine tuning necessary for the concert artist.

It is important to work with teachers who inspire your playing and allow you to grow into your own style and identity. A teacher whose reputation is respected in the arts management field also can be very helpful in getting your career off to a good start.

In order to get into the system of the concert performance, you must be self-motivated and totally committed. You must do everything you can to get exposure and experience. You must seek out the competitions that will get you a scholarship to a conservatory in order to obtain recognition as a concert artist.

It is very rare for anyone to succeed in the concert field without a formal education. Talent scouts are everywhere: teachers, administrators, and arts managers. A competition can win you a recital sponsored by an important association or guild. That, in turn, can win you a favorable press review and recognition from an arts manager with a contract for a concert tour. Competitions, grants, awards, scholarships, arts managers, and supportive organizations are listed in *Musical America, International Directory of Performing Arts, Music Industry Directory,* and *Sterns Performing Arts Directory.*

A concert might pay you $1,000 or more. That doesn't include room and board, travel, or agent commissions. What seems like a lot of money really isn't. You'll have to find a way of supplementing your income until the money gets better.

Be sure that you are willing to live out of a suitcase before you choose the concert circuit as your career goal. A successful concert artist sometimes does 60 to 100 concerts a year. That adds up to a great deal of traveling.

However, the performance and the traveling are only part of it. You may have played a beautiful concerto, but the final show for approval is at the cocktail reception afterward. Can you socialize? Do you enjoy meeting and talking with people? A good personality is very important to a successful concert career. Many concert artists make guest appearances with symphony orchestras. Concert artists also teach privately and are on staff with conservatories, colleges, and universities. Strong interpersonal skills are important in each of these situations.

Organizations to Contact

Concert solo instruments are generally limited to piano, violin, cello, organ, harp, guitar, horns, woodwinds, and voice. Concert ensembles include two pianos, harp ensembles, string quartets, woodwind and brass ensembles. The concert Artists Guild presents soloists and ensembles in a debut recital with press coverage. For audition information write to Concert Artists Guild, Inc., 850 Seventh Avenue, New York, NY 10019 .

The Interlochen Center for the Arts, P.O. Box 199, Interlochen, MI 49643-0199, offers young musicians the opportunity of intensive study in summer workshop programs.

Young Concert Artists is a nonprofit management organization that encourages outstanding young solo musicians and helps launch their careers. For audition information write to Young Concert Artists, Inc., 250 West 57th Street, New York, NY 10019.

Young Musicians Foundation encourages young musicians in the Southwest by offering them performance opportunities and financial assistance. For information and application, write to Young Musicians Foundation, 195 South Beverly Drive, Beverly Hills, CA 90212.

Other organizations that may provide you with helpful information include the following:

American Federation of Musicians
1501 Broadway
New York, NY 10036

National Federation of Music Clubs
1336 North Delaware Street
Indianapolis, IN 46202

American Symphony Orchestra League
777 Fourteenth Street, N.W.
Suite 500
Washington, D.C. 20005

The National Orchestra Association
475 Riverside Drive
Suite 249
New York, NY 10115

Chamber Music America
545 Eighth Avenue
New York, NY 10018

OPERA

Opera is an art form that combines voice (solo and chorus), theater, ballet, and a symphony orchestra with old world traditions and new world technology in a grand performance, a performance that finishes to standing ovations. According to the Central Opera Service, there are 209 opera companies and musical theater companies (light opera and operetta) with budgets over $100,000, 658 with budgets under that, and 418 college and university workshops.

According to the National Endowment for the Arts, opera, like symphony and chamber orchestras, is subsidized by foundations and grants. A survey of 331 opera, symphony, and chamber companies showed that 40 percent of the costs were defrayed by the price of admission and 60 percent were covered by foundations; corporations; private contributions; and city, state, and federal funding.

In one season, the Metropolitan Opera produces 20 to 25 operas in 265 performances, and the San Francisco Opera produces 14 operas in 75 regular performances and 16 spring performances. Smaller companies produce only three or four operas in a season.

Opera, whether grand or lyric (light), tragic or comic, takes the combined talents of singers, musicians, dancers, conductors, prompters, stage directors, choreographers, vocal coaches, accompanists, stage managers, librarians, makeup artists, hair stylists, scenic designers, set builders, property managers, costume designers, wardrobe managers, and lighting specialists.

Smaller opera companies hire well-known singers to perform the principal roles, and that makes it very difficult for young singers to get leading parts. Singers who are starting a career in opera should seek out competitions, apprenticeship programs, chorus work, and workshops. The competition is very intense. Working and studying in Europe is a good way to gain experience, exposure, and repertoire. Working in a chorus is steady and may give you a chance to perform a minor part. Much can be learned from watching a star perform, and being in the chorus as part of the performance is a great advantage.

The national pay scale for chorus work in 1990 was $435 per week. The scale for principal roles was $561 (3 performances a week) and can vary from one area to another.

Operatic Training

Aspiring opera singers should begin general music studies at an early age; vocal training should begin at a more mature age, usually in the teens, and continue throughout the career. A good background in music, languages, and piano is very important.

Besides a private voice teacher to help develop technique, a singer also needs to study with a vocal coach to develop repertoire. A singer is a musician whose instrument is the voice. Like a concert instrumentalist, he or she should seek out a formal education and studies in language, sight-singing, harmony, and theory, as well as coaching in early Italian art songs, German lieder, and English and French art songs. Operas are written in Italian, French, English, German, and Russian. An opera singer usually speaks more than one language and should be familiar with several others. Dance, acting, and other theater skills are also necessary. Opera workshops, vocal ensemble, and solo recitals are all part of the preparation for a career in opera.

Female singers are classified as soprano, mezzo-soprano, and contralto. Men are classified as tenor, baritone, and bass (basso). Further classifications are coloratura, lyric, spinto, robusto, dramatic, and basso profundo.

A singer must have a good-quality voice, good intonation, phrasing, musicality, and style, as well as a technique that displays vocal control, agility, and dynamics. A singer must also possess stage presence, charisma, and the ability to work well with others and follow directions. Most importantly, a singer must have patience. A voice that is pushed before its time can end a career before it starts. A singer should know his or her voice and concentrate on developing the repertoire that shows off its style and ability.

Finding Teachers, Grants, and Scholarships

The Central Opera Service publishes *Career Guide for the Young American Singer* and its addendum, which is a yearly update. The guide lists names, addresses, contacts, and rules for grants, study abroad, American and international competitions, apprenticeship programs, and workshops. Central Opera Services also publishes *Opera/Musical Theater Companies and Workshops in the United States and Canada*. Membership information and publications are available from the Central Opera Service, c/o The Metropolitan Opera, Lincoln Center, New York, NY 10023.

The Metropolitan National Council sponsors an audition program seeking potential talent for the future. There are 17 regions in the United States, Canada, and Australia, each divided into districts. Anyone can enter, with sponsorship from a teacher, choir director, or vocal coach. The age requirements are 19 to 33 for women and 20 to 33 for men. The applicant must be able to sing five arias in more than one language. The finals are held at the Metropolitan Opera at Lincoln Center, in New York. Winners receive grants to further their studies, as well as valuable exposure and credibility. For more details write to the Metropolitan National Council, Lincoln Center, New York, NY 10023, or call 212-870-4515.

The National Association of Teachers of Singing (NATS) is an organization made up of approximately 4,500 voice teachers throughout the country. Rules for joining NATS are strict, and its teacher members adhere to a code of ethics. A singer wishing to find a NATS teacher can do so by contacting the main office in Jacksonville, Florida.

NATS sponsors an artists competition that awards a $5,000 first prize and a $2,500 second prize, as well as an appearance at a workshop (for added exposure). An applicant may or may not be a professional, but must have studied with a NATS teacher for at least two years. The competition starts at a district level, goes to 14 regional levels, and then on to the finals, which are held every 18 months (July or December) at the NATS convention.

The NATS bulletin is available to nonmembers and is published five times a year. It contains information about competitions, workshops, and seminars; articles on voice and opera; and book, music, and record reviews. For subscription information and a list of NATS teachers, write to: The National Association of Teachers of Singing, 2800 University Blvd., N., J.U. Station, Jacksonville, FL 32211.

New York Singing Teachers Association (NYSTA) is similar to NATS, except that it concentrates on singers in the New York area. Most singing teachers in and around New York belong to both NYSTA and NATS. NYSTA sponsors three competitions a year: The Genevieve B. Gauman Recital Award, the Young Artists Awards, and the Music Theater Competition. NYSTA also presents an art song symposium, music theater symposium, and a composers showcase. For more information, write to: New York Singing Teachers Association, 884 West End Avenue, New York, NY 10025.

Opera America has a membership of 123 opera companies: 102 in the United States, 10 in Canada, and 11 in Europe and Australia. Their publication, *Profile,* contains a list of the opera companies. It can be purchased from their Washington office: Opera America, 777 14th Street, N.W., Suite 520, Washington, DC 20005. Opera America also publishes a *Singers Guide to the Professional Opera Companies.* The guide lists more than 150 training, apprentice, and artists-in-residence programs at 98 opera companies. It also contains information on competitions, casting, and other opportunities. Singers working in a member company have the chance to network with the other member companies.

Singers working in opera usually belong to the American Guild of Musical Artists (1727 Broadway, New York, NY 10019-5214). Singers working in musical theater usually belong to Actors Equity Association (165 West 46th Street, New York, NY 10036).

The American Institute of Musical Studies (AIMS) presents the AIMS Graz Experience each year in Graz, Austria. This includes the Summer Vocal Institute, the AIMS Chorale, and the AIMS

Graz Festival Orchestra. Advertisements are placed in *Opera News, Musical America, Opera Canada,* and *International Musician,* as well as in other trade journals. Auditions are held for singers, pianists, and instrumentalists. AIMS also sponsors seminars and workshops in the United States and publishes *Towards a Career in Europe.* For further information and to be placed on the mailing list, write to AIMS, 3500 Maple Avenue, Suite 120, LB 22, Dallas, TX 75219-3901.

CONDUCTORS

A conductor is a total musician, yet the only musician who can't create music without the orchestra. Singers can take a deep breath and let out a song; instrumentalists can pick up their instruments and make music, but the conductor must have an orchestra to lead.

Standing on a podium in front of a symphony orchestra is a thrilling experience. Taking leadership of a hundred personalities and temperaments and directing them according to one interpretation of the music requires great strength. A conductor must have a good personality, leadership skills, and charisma. In addition to command and technique of the baton, a conductor must have an excellent sense of rhythm, a good ear, a knowledge of all the orchestral instruments, a large repertoire, and a good feel for all of the music styles.

A knowledge of the piano is important in order to work on scores, and playing an instrument affords the conductor the chance to be part of an orchestra as a musician, and also to learn from within. Many famous conductors started their careers as string players or assistant conductors.

Training

A conductor usually starts studying at an early age, learning an instrument and the basics of music. University or conservatory training is essential. A school with a good orchestra and many smaller groups can give a student much experience at conducting.

There are many competitions for conductors, and getting exposure can lead to acceptance in a conductor-training program. Competitions are listed in *Musical America: International Directory of the Performing Arts* (825 Seventh Avenue, New York, NY 10019).

There are thousands of orchestras, both nationally and internationally. Some offer apprenticeships and positions as assistant conductors. Opera and ballet companies, musical theater, Broadway and off-Broadway shows, regional companies, dinner theaters, and summer stock all have orchestras that need conductors. The Central Opera Service lists approximately 1,100 opera/musical theater companies and workshops in the United States and Canada. *The Backstage Handbook for Performing Artists* has a list of regional, dinner, and summer theaters. *The Chronicle of Higher Education* (1255 Twenty-Third Street, N.W., Washington, DC 20037) has a classified section with ads seeking conductors to fill vacancies with college and university orchestras.

Conductors compose, arrange, and orchestrate. Many jobs need the services of a multitalented conductor who can write and accompany singers in rehearsal. A conductor or musical director must wear many hats. Besides the obvious demands on talent and leadership, he or she must also be able to manage the orchestra's business affairs, helping to plan the budget, scheduling programs, hosting visiting artists, and socializing at cocktail parties. Fundraising is a very important part of the job. Every orchestra needs money to function, and the conductor, being the focal point of the orchestra, must have a warm and open personality in order to attract these funds.

Working as an opera coach can give a conductor the chance to learn the repertoire and get the experience of conducting for a small opera company. Eventually a conductor can work his or her way up to an assistantship in a light opera company or musical theater company.

Conductors can also find work in churches and synagogues as choir directors. And there are many community and school projects that require the services of a good choral director.

Some conductors travel as guest conductors, and others stay with one orchestra. Salaries can range from about $7,500 to over $100,000 a year. That includes recordings and guest appearances with other orchestras.

Getting the right exposure is important in getting an arts manager to sign a conductor. When conductors are seasoned and ready, they sometimes hire a hall and an orchestra in New York, invite the press, and present themselves in a debut performance.

MUSICAL THEATER

The musical theater requires the same high caliber musician as do the symphony and the opera. In fact, many Broadway pit musicians are, or have been, members of a symphony and/or opera orchestra. The musical producer hires a contractor, who in turn hires the musicians. Knowing the contractor can be advantageous when trying to get work in a pit orchestra.

Theatrical Index (Price-Berkley Publication, 888 Eighth Avenue, New York, NY 10019) maintains a list of future productions, along with the names, addresses, and phone numbers of the producers. It lists the Broadway and off-Broadway productions, the national companies, and the tours. Musicians, singers, conductors, arrangers, and orchestrators alike should find this weekly publication very useful.

Regional theater has grown throughout the country and has opened up many opportunities for composers and performing artists. *Backstage Handbook for Performing Artists* has a list of regional theaters.

Additional Organizations

Other helpful organizations include the following:

Professional Women Singers Association Inc.
P.O. Box 884
Planetarium Station
New York, NY 10024

American Harp Society
6331 Quebec Drive
Hollywood, CA 90068-2831

Conductors Guild Inc.
P.O. Box 3361
West Chester, PA 19381

CHAPTER 3

THE MUSIC CREATOR

THE COMPOSER

Writing serious music today is a difficult way to make a living. Few composers of serious contemporary music earn a living strictly as composers. There are, however, foundations that give grants and awards to composers.

A good source of information on foundations is the Foundation Center. There are over 17,000 active foundations in the United States. There are two Foundation national libraries and two Foundation field offices in the United States. The Foundation Center also supplies its publications and supplemental resources to cooperating collections in over 170 public, university, government, and foundation libraries in all 50 states, Australia, Canada, Mexico, Puerto Rico, the Virgin Islands, Great Britain, and Japan. A simple phone call will tell you where to find the collection nearest you (1-800-424-9836).

One good source of grants is the National Endowment for the Arts (NEA). In 1989, the NEA music program received a total of 1,766 applications and awarded 756 grants totaling slightly over 12 million dollars. The grants went to orchestras; chamber, New Music, and jazz ensembles; choruses; composers; and music fes-

33

tivals. In the same year, the NEA awarded 200 grants, totaling 4.2 million dollars, to opera–musical theater for new American works. Literature and applications can be obtained from their office: NEA, Music Program, Room 702, 1100 Pennsylvania Avenue, Washington, DC 20506.

Meet the Composer is a national composer service organization founded in 1974 to foster the creation, performance, and recording of music by American composers, and to develop new audiences for contemporary music. Meet the Composer awards grants for composer fees to nonprofit organizations that perform, present, or commission the works of composers sponsored by MTC. MTC programs include the Composers Performance Fund and Affiliate Network, Orchestra Residencies Program, the Composer/Choreographer Project, Meet the Composer/Reader's Digest Commissioning Program, and Jazz Program. MTC also publishes two handbooks: *Commissioning Music* and *Composers in the Marketplace: How to Earn a Living Writing Music.* For information, write: Meet the Composer Inc., 2112 Broadway, Suite 505, New York, NY 10023.

The American Society of Composers, Authors and Publishers (ASCAP) and Broadcast Music Inc. (BMI) also award grants to composers. There are many organizations and associations that promote and encourage new composers. *Music America International Directory of Performing Arts* lists grants, awards, and competitions. Your local public library should have a copy. *Music Industry Directory,* Marques Publications, and *Sterns Performing Arts Directory* are two other sources of information.

A composer is the creative force in music and must have a good imagination and understanding of the emotional effects of music. A thorough knowledge of harmony and theory, familiarity with sounds and ranges of instruments, and an understanding of the techniques of composing and arranging are essential. Composers write symphony and chamber music, opera, choral music, church music, ballet, and theater music; they also write for commercials, industrials, feature films and television. Composers create everything from band music to jingles to popular music.

Teaching in a college, university, or conservatory is one of the best sources of income for a composer. The pleasant atmosphere is conducive to creativity, and the availability of musicians to play the compositions is a great asset. A composer can also earn a living by teaching privately; by arranging music for shows, singers, and acts; or by working as an accompanist, conductor, choir director, vocal coach, or church musician.

The Computer Age

The computer has become an important tool for the composer. In fact, in some areas of music it has taken over completely. A computer and several synthesizers can imitate the sound of an entire orchestra, with the added advantage that electronic sounds have an infinite range of colors. This new technology has revolutionized the music industry. A composer must be familiar with the techniques and equipment used to create these new sounds.

New England Digital (NED) has created an instrument called the Synclavier. It is a highly sophisticated computer/sequencer/synthesizer/sampler and digital recorder. It has become an important tool in postproduction work for film and television. It is also used to create a music sound track without the use of live musicians.

Kurzweil, and synthesis pioneer Robert Moog, developed an instrument called the Kurzweil 250. It is a keyboard/sampler that can duplicate the sound of strings, horns, piano, bass, drums, and many other instruments and sounds.

Other companies such as Yamaha, Roland, AKAI, Emulater, and Korg have also created instruments that can produce thousands of sounds at the touch of a finger. Many of these synthesizer manufacturers, computer companies, and software companies employ musicians and composers with computer backgrounds for research and development, sales and promotion, and education and demonstration.

Many composers have put together what is called a MIDI (Musical Instrument Digital Interface) studio in their homes. Some use it as a composer's workstation, programming the score and sounds onto a floppy disk, and recording it as a demo. At a later date, they bring the disk to a full-blown studio to record the master. Again, all this is managed without the use of any live musicians. However, many composers and producers mix the sound of live musicians with their electronic sounds. It's all a question of budget and creative preferences. Presently the trend in Hollywood is to go back to using live musicians and large orchestras for feature films.

Some composers invest a great deal of money in their workstations and create a multitrack home studio capable of producing a broadcast-quality finished product. A home studio can cost anywhere from $10,000 to $150,000. However, a Synclavier alone can cost from $75,000 to $500,000, and you still need a mixing console, a multitrack recording deck, and a lot of other equipment. A composer has to be willing to invest a lot of money into this type of equipment.

More important than money is time. The computer, the program, the synthesizer, the sampler, the mixing console, the recording deck, and all the other pieces of equipment that go into a studio have to be studied, for each has its own technology. And, although these high-tech instruments can create great sounds and interesting sequences, it still takes a composer to turn these sounds and sequences into a musical composition.

There are rewards for those who succeed. A musician who is skilled in computer/synthesis technology (sometimes referred to as a programmer) can earn anywhere from minimum wage to several thousand dollars per week, depending on his or her stature in the industry, and the project and/or artist with whom they work.

Many local schools have courses, workshops, and seminars in this new technology. In New York there is the New School for Social Research, The Guitar Study Center, Center for Electronic Music, and the Center for Media Arts. The local music dealer who sells this type of equipment can be another good source of information.

For books on this subject, check *The Mix Bookshelf, Mix Magazine, Alexander Books, Keyboard Magazine,* and *Electronic Musician.*

THE ARRANGER/ORCHESTRATOR

A composer creates the theme and melody, the harmony, and the countermelody (counterpoint). An arranger adopts and prepares this already written melody and harmony for a performance, with a beginning (intro), middle, repeats, modulations, variations, and an ending. The orchestrator scores the arrangement, dividing the voices and assigning them to various instruments.

An orchestrator must know the range of instruments and how to blend them for specific sounds and effects. In some instances the composer, arranger, and orchestrator can be the same person. Most times, however, the work is contracted out to two or three different people.

In film scoring, a composer is hired to write the main theme and underscore. A lyricist will be hired if the producer wants words set to the main theme. In some films, songwriting teams are hired, in addition to the composer, to create specific songs for the film. An arranger and/or the composer then synchronizes the music to match the film's hit points (specific points of action); they arrange each music cue to fit its specific mood and duration in time. This is all calculated from the timing sheets (a feet and frame readout of the film supplied by the music editor). The tempo is then translated into a click track, a special metronome used for film scoring. An orchestrator is called in to score the composition for each music cue, a copyist copies the music from the score and notates it onto individual charts (music paper) for each instrument. Then an orchestra and a conductor go into a recording studio, called a scoring stage. And, finally, through this combination of artistry and technology, the movie comes alive with music.

FILM AND TELEVISION

Major studios, producers, and networks have a music director. The person who holds this executive position usually has a music background and comes from the A&R (artist & repertoire) department of a record company. The music director oversees all the music business and production for the company. Generally speaking, he or she does not have creative input, but the music director is familiar with artists, composers, and songwriters, and sometimes is called upon for an expert opinion.

"Music supervisor" is a fairly recent title in the film industry; it started in the early 1980s. Supervisors are similar to the music director, except that music supervisors do have creative input. This is a free-lance position, and music supervisors generally work on one specific film project. They are responsible for setting up budgets and schedules, negotiating with composers, lyricists, songwriters, and artists. Music supervisors act as liaison between the producer, the director, the composer, the film editor, and the music editor. Their duties include handling all the paperwork with regard to copyrights, licensing, reuse, and contracts. Music supervisors help select songs, as well as coordinate and produce all the music.

Another important position is that of music editor. This person works very closely with the composer. Music editors are usually film editors who may or may not have a background in music, but have a good feel for and understanding of music. Along with the director, producer, film editor, and composer, music editors attend the spotting session to determine where the music will be placed in the film. Music editors take notes regarding the music cues; they prepare timing sheets and click tracks for the composer.

If the final cut is on video, then a time code (hours-minutes-seconds-frames) is "burned" into the picture and onto one of the audio tracks, for use as a reference guide. Sometimes music editors are called upon to prepare a "temp track"—a temporary music track made from already existing songs and music cues that are similar to the final music. Temp tracks serve as a working guide for editors and directors.

Music editors belong to the Motion Picture and Videotape Editors Guild, 7715 Sunset Boulevard, Hollywood, CA 90046.

A good guide to motion picture and TV development and production companies is the *Hollywood Creative Directory,* 451 Kelton Avenue, Los Angeles, CA 90024.

PRODUCTION MUSIC LIBRARIES

Approximately 25 to 30 production companies produce music that is not "original," not written for a specific project. Seventeen of these companies are members of the Production Music Library Association of America (1619 Broadway, New York, NY 10019). The type of music they publish is also referred to as library music or stock music, and it came into existence in 1927.

Some companies have composers on staff, and others hire them on a free-lance basis. Free-lance composers are sometimes paid for the composition up front, or they work on speculation. Use of the music is called a "needle drop" or "drop," and the user must pay a fee which is split evenly by the production company and the composer. If the music is broadcast on TV or radio, it then generates an ASCAP, BMI, or SESAC royalty. Composers can earn up to $100,000 or more per year depending on if, and how, their music is used.

The music is written according to certain specifications, such as romantic moods, chase music, fanfares, dream sequences, and so on. Sometimes the music is composed to specific lengths, like 15 seconds or 5 minutes. The music is written for small combos on up to symphony orchestras, and it covers all styles, such as jazz, country, and pop. The music is used by audiovisual companies, industrial producers, schools, broadcasters, as well as film and TV producers.

BACKGROUND MUSIC

There are three major companies that supply what is called "background music," sometimes referred to as "wallpaper music." You've experienced it many times—in a doctor's waiting room, in an elevator, in a restaurant, and in the work place. It is broadcast via satellite to a location, or purchased as an on-location service, with the music company supplying a tape deck and special cassettes.

These companies sometimes license original works from composers; however, the piece must be recorded in a professional studio using acoustic instruments. Homemade MIDI/synthesizer recordings are not accepted. The background music company generally hires a production company to record songs for their catalog of standard and contemporary songs. The production company then hires the orchestrator, the arranger, the musicians, and the recording studio. Vocalists are never used.

As part of their service, the background music company pays the licensing fee to ASCAP, BMI, and SESAC, who in turn pay the composers a royalty for the use of their music. Approximately eight producers, in about five or six cities, produce this type of music. Their catalog includes small combos as well as large orchestras, and the style of music is categorized as contemporary classic, new age, light jazz, soft rock, and adult contemporary.

GETTING INTO THE INDUSTRY

If you want to be a composer, try to get a job with a producer of background music or demonstration records, or anything that will give you the opportunity to be around composers and orchestrators. Do copy work or menial office chores, even sweep the floors. You may hear of a new producer looking for an arranger, or an orchestrator, or there may be some overflow work you can handle. If you are not in the office, or the studio, they'll never know you, and you'll never know them. Many composers get their break by orchestrating for established composers. If you're working in a studio or have a home studio, record some samples of your own themes and orchestrations; then use the tape as a demo to show your talents. Keep it short.

There are also opportunities to gain experience as a volunteer. Producers of public affairs commercials always need talented and eager composers who are willing to donate their time and expertise. Look in the trade papers, like *Backstage, Variety, Show Business,* and the *Hollywood Reporter.*

Student film projects quite often need music, and working for a student director will give you a sample of your work. Also, you will be meeting the future producers and directors who will one day be creating major feature films and television. Check with a college or university film department for opportunities.

Many film and television composers use the Schillinger system of composition. It might be helpful to study with someone who uses that approach. Studying with a composer or an arranger who is on the scene can give you many tips.

Belonging to the Musicians Union and to other professional organizations should get you some leads. Once you've got your first assignment, you will have a sample of your work and the proof of your worth.

THE COPYIST

Copyists free-lance or work for a copy service or a publishing company. A knowledge of music, transposition, and music notation is necessary. Since copying is the drawing of notes on the staff (or stave), it requires good penmanship. If you enjoy this type of work, you might consider working for a publisher. Copyists, transcribers, and autographers are all needed to prepare sheet music for printers. There are also computer programs capable of printing music. Music copyists should also familiarize themselves with these computer techniques.

Pay scales for copy work are per-page and per-hour, depending on the nature of the work. The AFM (American Federation of Musicians) Phonograph Record Labor Agreement publishes the following scales:

> Composing and arranging are considered creative skills; therefore, the fees are left to the individuals doing the work. However, an arranger's fee cannot be less than the orchestrator's fee. Where the arranger is also the orchestrator, he or she will receive the orchestration fee in addition to the arranging fee.

The 1990 hourly rate for an orchestrator was $27.56, and the page rate was $17.12 for ten-line score paper (according to AFM's

1990 list). The hourly rate for a copyist was $18.98, and the page rate varied according to the part. All rates are variable according to style and specifications of the music. Orchestrating and copying for television, theater, and feature film each have different pay rates.

You must have samples of your work to present to music houses, producers, composers, orchestrators, arrangers, sheet music publishers, songwriters, singers, and anyone else who might need your services.

You may want to join the music copyist organization:

American Society of Music Copyists
P.O. Box 41
Radio City Station
New York, NY 10101

ADVERTISING MUSIC

Writing advertising music is an art and trade in itself. Most advertising music is produced in New York; Los Angeles and Chicago also have a good share of the business. However, there are other jingle producers all over the country.

A music production company, sometimes called a music house, is usually responsible for the jingle and the scoring. Most music houses are self-contained; the owners are the composers, songwriters, instrumentalists, singers, producers, arrangers, and contractors. The copy work is sometimes done by someone else; however, music houses tend to use the same people over and over again.

Some music production companies maintain their own recording studio and compose and produce everything in-house. A job with a music house can give you the opportunity to be in the right place at the right time. If you can get some of the overflow to write, or get to perform on the demos, you can build a reputation for yourself and collect samples of your work. If you play an instrument or sing, working on the bread-and-butter jobs can give you leads and sustain you as you make your rounds with your presentation reel.

From Concept to Airplay

An advertising agency creative director (CD) gets an assignment to create a concept for a new client's product. The CD then assigns the project to one or more creative teams under his or her supervision. The teams consist of an art director and a copywriter. Each team comes up with several ideas for radio and television commercials, and they all need music.

All the concepts for the ad campaign are presented, and the best idea is then selected. At that point a producer is brought in to coordinate the entire production of the spots. The producer may be someone on staff or a free-lance person. The producer, creative director, art director, and copywriter (who is also the lyricist) decide what type of music and which composer to use. They then call on their music director—if the agency is large enough to have one—to help with their decision. The music director, or the producer, has a file of composer's tapes, from which they select the style they like best.

Next, they call in several composers to create a demo and a budget. There is usually a small fee for this service. The composers use either the storyboard or the video as a guide. In most cases the composers must present their ideas the next day, and, of course, the best one is selected.

Musicians are multitalented, and many of today's jingle writers have worked as advertising copywriters, producers, or art directors. A job with an advertising agency or a music house can open many doors for an aspiring jingle writer.

Good sources of information on the advertising industry are the *Madison Avenue Handbook* (Peter Glenn Publications, New York) and the *Backstage TV Film & Tape Production Directory* (Backstage Publications, New York). Each lists advertising agencies, film producers, TV producers, and music houses. *Through the Jingle Jungle,* by Steve Karmen, Billboard Books, New York, is also suggested reading for those interested in advertising music.

Industrials

An industrial is a film, video, musical theater piece, or musical revue that advertises a product or a company. It could be a series of songs about a corporation, a state, a car, or a beverage. Very often composers, arrangers, and copyists are used to write and produce the original music. *New York Casting and Survival Guide* (Peter Glenn Publications, New York) publishes a list of industrial producers.

MUSICAL THEATER

In the 1920s through the 1940s, Broadway, "The Great White Way," played host to composers like Cole Porter, George Gershwin, Jerome Kern, and Irving Berlin. These composers left a legacy of songs that are part of America's everyday life, songs that are still played and sung all over the world. There's no excitement like a Broadway show, the thrill of opening night, and the applause that's heard around the world if the show is a hit.

Songs for Broadway musical theater are created through the collaboration of a composer and a lyricist. An arranger then expands the songs into dance numbers, chorus numbers, overtures, reprises, and whatever else is needed. The music is then orchestrated and copied. Finally, after many months of rehearsal, a conductor directs the pit musicians and the stage actors through an opening night performance that will either make or break the show.

Because of the tremendous production costs involved in creating a Broadway show, few producers are willing to take a chance on young, unproven composers. So, for new composers, off-off Broadway, off-Broadway, showcases, revues, and regional theaters are the best venues for getting attention. Many hit musicals are now getting their start in regional theater.

Creating a Show

How would you create a Broadway show? Find a book, a lyricist, and a playwright, and just start composing the songs. When you've finished, get financial backers. To do this, put together a backers' audition tape, a demonstration tape with all the songs in sequence. Gather a group of potential backers to listen to you, with your tape player running. You and your partners, or professional actors, narrate the story line, or read the lines from the script, and play the songs as needed. If the backers and the producer like it, you are on your way to becoming a musical theater composer.

How to you find a lyricist? By working in and around the Broadway scene! Working for a producer, or even a literary agent, can afford you the opportunity to meet theater people. Actors often write plays; maybe that's a way to find a good story to convert into a musical.

Organizations to Contact

Organizations such as The Songwriters Guild of America, ASCAP, BMI, and the Dramatists Guild have seminars for composers and lyricists of the musical theater. The NEA awards grants for special theater projects, and there are many organizations that help and encourage new writers.

The Dramatists Guild, Inc. (234 W. 44th Street, New York, NY 10036) is a professional organization whose membership consists of playwrights, lyricists, and composers. The guild sponsors workshops and symposia across the country, in which experienced professionals discuss various aspects of writing for the theater. The guild has a special contract form that members can use in drawing up contracts between themselves and producers. In addition, the guild publishes the *Dramatists Guild Quarterly* and a newsletter.

THE SONGWRITER

The song is where it all begins; without a song there would be no singer, no musician, and thus no music business. There are approximately three thousand music publishers listed in Billboard's 1990 *International Buyers Guide,* and every one of them has songwriters knocking on their door.

It all began in turn-of-the-century New York City, on a street called Tin Pan Alley. Songwriters went from publisher to publisher with their songs, hoping that one of them would sell and become a hit. It's no different today. From New York to Nashville to Los Angeles, wherever a publisher sets up shop, newcomers try to sell their songs. The styles may change, the song forms may change, but the demand for good music never ceases.

Making Contacts

There are several good ways for songwriters to make contacts. Songwriting clubs exist all around the country. Their members all share the same interest in writing a song that gets published and recorded, becomes a hit, and makes its author rich and famous. In some areas there are nightclubs that showcase songwriters. Check the yellow pages, or ask musicians at local clubs. You can also get information from the music department of the college or university in your area. The trade papers, like *Billboard* and *Cashbox,* are very good sources of information. If you get frustrated, make a long distance call to one of them. Someone will help you.

If you are serious about songwriting, you should belong to several songwriters' organizations in order to make contacts, find collaborators, and get information. Groups like The Songwriter's Guild of America (SGA), Nashville Songwriters Association International (NSAI), ASCAP (American Society of Composers, Authors and Publishers), and BMI (Broadcast Music Inc.) are good choices. They all have pamphlets and booklets to help you learn the business of songwriting. They also have seminars and workshops to help you network and learn the craft of songwriting.

Financial Arrangements

Songwriters free-lance or work on staff with publishers. Some songwriters are signed to one publisher, and everything they write belongs to that company. Others are on a first-refusal basis, which means the publisher has the option of buying or refusing a song. If the publisher refuses to buy it, then the songwriter is free to sell to another publisher.

A publisher buys a song by signing a contract, usually giving the songwriter a small advance, and agreeing to pay royalties. Staff writers are paid a small salary that is considered an advance on their royalties. Royalties are fees based on record sales, sheet music sales, airplay, and public performances.

Organizations like ASCAP, BMI, and SESAC collect fees from radio and TV broadcasters, restaurants, clubs, hotels, and whoever else uses music for profit. Each group has its own special surveys and complicated formulas for determining fees, which are divided proportionately according to the rate at which each composition is played. The royalty is divided into two parts paid directly by the licensing agency. Part of the royalty goes to the publisher and the other goes to the writer or writers.

Organizations like the Harry Fox Agency collect mechanical royalties from record companies. A mechanical is a phonograph record, cassette tape, or a compact disk (CD). Under the old copyright law, the royalty rate was two cents per song. This royalty would be collected by the Harry Fox Agency and distributed accordingly. The 1976 Copyright Act created the Copyright Royalty Tribunal (CRT), which is made up of five commissioners appointed by the president. Legislation is pending to reduce the number of CRT commissioners from five to three. The purpose of the tribunal is to adjust the royalty rate. As of January 1990, the rate is 5.7 cents or 1.1 cents per minute, whichever is greater. The CRT will meet every two years through 1997 to adjust the mechanical royalty rate. However, the rate may never fall below 5 cents, nor increase more than 25 percent in any two-year period.

A song has to sell a lot of records, cassettes, CDs, or sheet music and get a large amount of radio and TV exposure in order for a writer to make a substantial amount of money. Even if a song is a hit, it takes a long time for the money to filter down through the system into the writer's pocket. At one time, licensing agencies (ASCAP, BMI) gave advances to publishers and songwriters, but because of legal difficulties, the practice of giving advances has been discontinued, except in cases of extreme hardship. And, according to the National Music Publishers Association, home taping currently accounts for more than a billion dollars in annual losses to the music industry internationally.

Where to Start

The three main music centers for songwriters are New York, Nashville, and Los Angeles. Some other markets are Toronto, Shreveport, Muscle Shoals, Chicago, Miami, Minneapolis, Atlanta, and Boston. However, before you move to a music center, be sure you have a job waiting for you or enough money saved to sustain yourself during your quest. Songwriters face stiff competition today. Many record and publishing companies use recording artists who write their own material, which leaves very little room for outside writers. If you sing or play an instrument, you might be able to get a job as an entertainer, but remember that many other songwriters will have the same idea.

Since there are more than enough songwriters showcasing their talents and seeking recognition, the likelihood of being paid for your talent is slim. You could end up pumping gas, waiting tables, or even going home broke and disillusioned. A better way to start might be to work in your home town, using the phone and mail to make some contacts with publishers. Then make a few visits to build your contacts. Once you've saved enough money to support yourself and have built some solid contacts, then consider relocating.

A songwriter needs instruments, reference materials, recording equipment, a typewriter, lead sheets (sheet music), copyrights, and demos—all of which are expensive. Phone calls, postage, stationery, and lunch dates can also be very costly.

Close association with other songwriters, publishers, artists, and producers is also essential for a songwriter to gain recognition. A songwriter must do homework to learn what type of music each publisher handles, who the professional manager is, what style of songs is selling, and which artists, producers, and record labels use outside material. An excellent guide for a songwriter,

Songwriters Market, is published yearly by Writer's Digest Books, 1507 Dana Avenue, Cincinnati, OH 45207.

Song festivals and contests are good ways of getting exposure. The annual Billboard Song Contest is one of the more popular ways to getting your song heard. For an application and information on fees and entry rules, write to:

Billboard Song Contest
P.O. Box 35346
Tulsa, OK 74153-0346.

COPYRIGHTS

To show ownership of a piece of music, you simply have to affix the copyright notice, which is a small *c* in a circle ©, the abbreviation COPR, or the word *copyright*. This information is followed by the year and the name of the copyright owner. (Example: ©1990 Bob Gerardi). Once a composition is fixed, as a lead sheet or a recording, it is automatically copyrighted. However, to file ownership and to protect the song, you must register it with the copyright office in Washington, D.C.

It is not possible to copyright song ideas or titles. A lead sheet showing the melody of the work, with or without the words, can be filed with Application PA, or a tape recording of the work can be filed with Application SR. Send the application, sample of the work, and a filing fee to the Register of Copyrights, Library of Congress, Washington, D.C. 20559. Then the song is registered and protected. If you're a prolific writer, copyrighting each song can be expensive. It would be advisable to wait until you have a group of songs and file them as a collection.

While filing a copyright is a simple procedure, copyright law is a very involved and complicated area. Learn as much about copyrights as possible, so that you can understand the law as it applies to you. Information, applications, and circulars are available from Copyright Office, Library of Congress, Washington, DC 20559.

An informative two-volume audio-book about the craft and business of songwriting is *Turn Songs into Gold,* by Norman Weiser, available from Halsey International, 24 Music Square West, Nashville, TN 37203.

ORGANIZATIONS FOR COMPOSERS AND SONGWRITERS

ASCAP
American Society of Composers, Authors and Publishers
One Lincoln Plaza
New York, NY 10023

BMI
Broadcast Music Inc.
320 West 57th Street
New York, NY 10019

SESAC
156 West 56th Street
New York, NY 10019

SGA
The Songwriters Guild of America
276 Fifth Avenue
New York, NY 10001

NAPM
The National Academy of Popular Music
875 Third Avenue
8th Floor
New York, NY 10022

NSAI
Nashville Songwriters Association International
1025 16th Avenue South
Suite 200
Nashville, TN 37212

The Foundation Center
79 Fifth Avenue
New York, NY 10003

or

312 Sutter Street
Third Floor
San Francisco, CA 94108

or

1001 Connecticut Avenue, N.W.
Washington, DC 20036

or

Kent H. Smith Library
1442 Hanna Building
Cleveland, OH 44115

NEA
National Endowment for the Arts
Music Program, Room 702
1100 Pennsylvania Avenue
Washington, DC 20506

American Composers Alliance
170 West 74th Street
New York, NY 10023

American Music Center
250 West 54th Street
New York, NY 10019

International Congress of Women in Music
P.O. Box 12164
La Crescenta, CA 91224-0864

International League of Women Composers
Southshore Road
Box 67 Pt. Penninsula
Three Mile Bay, NY 13693

League of Composers
International Society for Contemporary Music
c/o American Music Center
30 West 26th Street
New York, NY 10010-2011

National Association of Composers/USA
P.O. Box 49652
Barrington Station
Los Angeles, CA 90049

SAMPAC
Society of Advertising Music Producers, Arrangers, and Com-
    posers
P.O. Box 1514
Radio City Station
New York, NY 10101

The Society of Composers and Lyricists
2837 Hyperion Avenue
Los Angeles, CA 90027-2505

CHAPTER 4

MUSIC PUBLISHING

Music publishing can be categorized into three basic areas: (1) standard music publishing, which specializes in classical and serious contemporary music, (2) educational music publishing, which specializes in music instruction books and school band music, and (3) popular music publishing, which concentrates on new songs and the standard popular songs of the past that are played on the radio, TV, records, and in film.

Music publishing consists of presenting music for sale to the public, in print or in sound. Printed music is sheet music or a collection of songs in book form; the sale of printed music profits the publisher and provides a royalty for the writer(s). Sound publication of music is music recorded and presented to the public as a cassette tape, a CD, or in a sound track; the sale of records also results in a profit for the record company and a royalty to the publisher and the writer(s). Record royalties are called mechanical fees. Broadcasting music over radio or TV, using it in a film, or performing it live, obligates you to pay a performance royalty to the publisher(s) and the writer(s).

Publishers are all over the country, but the main concentration is in the three music centers: New York, Nashville, and Los Angeles. Salaries in music publishing range from $20,000 (entry-level) to $100,000 per year or more depending on the job, the location, and the person's status in the industry.

PROFESSIONAL MANAGER

A professional manager is the person at a music publishing company who finds new material and promotes it. Depending on the size of the company, the professional manager may have many responsibilities. He or she is a combination of song-promoter and talent scout. Managers may listen to songs submitted through the mail, sit with songwriters and listen to their tapes, or attend live performances in search of new material and writers. Many large publishers have staff songwriters who present their compositions to the professional manager.

The professional manager must have a good ear for music, be tuned in to the everyday business of music, listen to the radio constantly, read the trade papers, and be familiar with the popular record charts. Perhaps the most important part of the job is the ability to hear a commercial song and know which recording artist is best suited to perform it. Many of today's popular artists write their own songs, and some even have their own publishing companies. Therefore, a professional manager must know which artists will consider performing someone else's material.

The professional manager also must be familiar with the company's catalog. Many of today's pop hits were written 5, 10, or 15 years ago. New arrangements of standards that were hits years ago often become new hits of today. Warner/Chappel Music, one of the largest publishers in the world, maintains a catalog of approximately 300,000 titles.

After listening to the numerous submissions, the professional manager reviews selected songs at a weekly meeting of the professional staff. The songs finally selected and signed are made into demos so that each of the professional managers can "pitch" them to a special artist. Getting a song to a recording artist can be a real challenge. Each artist is associated with a manager, an agent, a producer, a record company, a publishing company, an arranger/conductor/accompanist, and a band. A professional manager has to do a great deal of planning to find a way of getting a song to a particular artist. Sometimes the demo of the song is recorded with a sound similar to that of the artist in mind. Sometimes, when several artists are being considered, several versions of the song might be recorded.

The professional manager must be creative in directing the producer of the demos toward different styles. He or she must be familiar with the recording studio, musicians, singers, arrangers, and engineers. In some cases, professional managers produce the demos themselves. A professional manager must know how to budget a demo session and which arrangers, musicians, and singers to call for the session.

The professional manager is really a salesperson, selling songs, and he or she must have a good personality and strong contacts with producers, artists, and record companies. A manager's work never ends. Once the song is recorded and released, he or she must "work" the song to get other artists to include it on their upcoming albums. For example, suppose the original artist sold one million records of the song. Meanwhile nine other artists also recorded it on their albums, and they each sold one million records. The publisher and writer would then receive royalties from ten million records.

TRANSCRIBER

In order for the song to be made into a demo, copyrighted, and presented, a lead sheet (sheet music) must be prepared. A transcriber is hired to make the lead sheet. The transcriber may be on the staff, or work free-lance. He or she listens to the recorded music and writes the notes of the melody and harmony on music paper. A transcriber (similar to a copyist) must have a good knowledge of music notation, a good ear, and a neat and artistic penmanship. Courses in dictation and ear training can prepare a person to transcribe.

COPYRIGHT MANAGER

Once a song is published, it must be copyrighted. This is usually done by the copyright department manager, who may also be responsible for rights and permissions. A basic knowledge of copyright law and licensing procedures is necessary to do this job. A person seeking a career in music publishing should also be familiar with the functions of the Harry Fox Agency, ASCAP, BMI, and SESAC.

TAPE COPIER

Every music publisher has a small room where the tape copies are made. Sometimes a person breaking into the business is given the title of tape copier and is responsible for making the cassette tapes, which are called transfers or dubs.

More often, the professional manager makes the tape copy. A basic knowledge of recording techniques is needed to make transfers. As simple as this operation may seem, it takes time and care to be sure that the tape has been properly prepared and checked before it is sent out.

PREPARATION OF SHEET MUSIC

After a song has been recorded and begins to get airplay, the sheet music is prepared, especially if the song is on its way to becoming a hit. An arranger is hired to prepare a piano/voice and guitar arrangement of the song. In some companies the arranger is on staff, otherwise a free-lance arranger may be hired.

After the arrangement is completed, it is passed on to an editor who checks it for errors in notation and spelling. The editor must have a good knowledge of music notation, harmony, and theory and an understanding of the style of music he or she is working on. In the case of band and orchestra arrangements, the editor must be familiar with orchestration, transposition, and the ranges of instruments.

The manuscript is then passed on to the engraver, who will carve the music notes onto a plate, or to a typographer who types the music notes with a special typewriter or computer. An autographer uses a special pen to write the music by hand. When the sheet music is completed, a proofreader checks the music against the original manuscript, and sometimes the composer also proofs the music.

An artist designs the cover-coordinating color, photographs, and design. Finally, the printer manufactures the finished sheet music, which is then distributed to music stores and made available to the public.

ADVERTISING

The popularity of the record is what advertises a song; as record sales go up, so do sheet music sales. In the cases of concert music, educational music, and classical music, however, it takes planned advertising to gain public attention. An advertising specialist, together with a copywriter and layout artist, plans the campaign. Salespeople, lecturers, and clinicians bring the music into the field, show it, explain it, and demonstrate it. Everyone involved in the campaign must have a love and knowledge of music in order to properly represent it.

GETTING INTO PUBLISHING

According to Frank Military, Senior Vice-President, Warner/Chappel Music, industry executives are always looking for bright, young, talented people who are eager to learn. Although a person may know and love music, and be a musician and a songwriter, there are some other basic skills that can open the door to a career in music publishing.

The ability to type is very important. Copyright forms, letters, lyric sheets, contracts, and envelopes all require typing. Knowing how to type, operate a tape recorder, and work on a word processor or computer can play an important part in getting you that first job.

People in publishing are self-motivated and, in most cases, learn their trade on the job. There are, however, many schools that teach music and entertainment business. *Suber's Guide to MEI Schools* (music and entertainment industry schools) is available from Charles Suber and Associates, 600 South Dearborn Street, Chicago, IL 60605. The book is also available on a computer disk (Macintosh) and includes quarterly updates.

Another good source of information is the Music and Entertainment Industry Educators Association (MEIEA). For information write to Janet Nepkie, Music Department, State University College, Oneonta, NY 13820.

Trade Publications

Cashbox
157 West 57th Street
Suite 1402
New York, NY 10019

Billboard
1515 Broadway
New York, NY 10036

Records and Radio
1930 Century Park West
Los Angeles, CA 90067

Trade Organizations

Music Publishers' Association of the United States
130 West 57th Street
New York, NY 10019

National Music Publishers' Association
205 East 42nd Street
New York, NY 10017

Harry Fox Agency
205 East 42nd Street
New York, NY 10017

Tip Sheets

Song Plugger and Tune Smith
P.O. Box 3839
Hollywood, CA 90028

Parade of Stars
1201 16th Avenue South
Nashville, TN 37212
(only available to publishers)

New on the Charts
Music Business Reference, Inc.
70 Laurel Place
New Rochelle, NY 10801
(only available to professionals)

CHAPTER 5

PROFESSIONAL ORGANIZATIONS

Professional organizations give musicians, singers, and writers opportunities to meet and network with people who share common interests. These organizations help make the public aware of the needs of their members. They establish codes of ethics, working conditions, and standards of excellence. They franchise agents and negotiate wages, health, and pension benefits with employers. Many professional organizations maintain pension plans, health plans, and credit unions, and most keep members informed through their many publications. Professional organizations often offer grants, scholarships, and seminars to further educate and inform their members. They also work to protect artists' rights by representing them in Washington, D.C.

For example, The National Endowment for the Arts is presently under attack for funding controversial artwork. Of the 75,000 grants awarded in the NEA's 25 year history, only two dozen have sparked public debate. Yet critics have targeted the NEA for extinction. Since this would be a devastating loss to the arts community, professional organizations inform their membership and encourage them to write to their congressional representatives and senators in support of the NEA.

Another problem is the DAT (digital audiotape) recorders being manufactured by Sony. As mentioned before, billions of dollars in royalties are lost to analog home tape recording. A DAT recorder makes it possible to record perfect, distortion-free, first-generation copies of CD's and digital broadcasts, which would encourage even more people to make their own tapes at home, resulting in even more lost royalties for music creators. The National Music Publishers' Association (NMPA), the Songwriters Guild of America (SGA), and the American Society of Composers, Authors and Publishers (ASCAP), have formed the Copyright Coalition. The coalition has filed a class action suit against Sony, charging that the DAT recorders and blank DAT cassettes interfere with federal copyrights. The coalition is seeking a copying safeguard known as the Serial Copying Management System (SCMS). They are also trying to get a home-taping royalty bill passed, which would attach a surcharge to the hardware and the blank tapes. The surcharge would then be passed on to the music creators.

AMERICAN FEDERATION OF MUSICIANS OF THE UNITED STATES AND CANADA (AFM)

The American Federation of Musicians of the United States and Canada was founded in the late nineteenth century. It is one of the oldest of the performance unions. The AFM (1501 Broadway, New York, NY 10036) has approximately 200,000 members in about 464 locals throughout the United States and Canada, with its headquarters in New York City. Members are instrumentalists, arrangers, orchestrators, copyists, proofreaders, conductors, librarians, and vocalists.

The AFM represents musicians in phonograph, film, TV, and commercial recordings; radio and TV broadcasting; the concert field; musical theater; opera; ballet; ice shows; the circus; steady engagements and single engagements. The AFM and its locals set working conditions within their jurisdictions for minimum size of orchestra, wage scales, special fees for doubling, travel, overtime, and rehearsal fees.

Members pay their local an initiation fee plus yearly dues and small work dues from each job. The local, in turn, pays the AFM dues on behalf of the member. The AFM has its own contract forms both for steady and single engagements and represents the musician in cases of nonpayment. The AFM also franchises agents who must adhere to AFM rules and regulations regarding bookings, wages, and commissions.

There are restrictions for switching locals, so be sure of each local's regulations before you move. The AFM local near you should be listed in the phone book. However, if you write or call the AFM headquarters in New York, they will be happy to give you any information you need.

The official journal of the AFM is *International Musician*. It is also available to nonmembers; it contains important news items, employment opportunities, and general information for the musician. In addition, each local publishes its own newsletter.

ASSOCIATED ACTORS AND ARTISTES OF AMERICA (AAAA)

The Actors' Equity Association, The American Federation of Television and Radio Artists, The American Guild of Musical Arts, The American Guild of Variety Artists, and the Screen Actors Guild comprise the four A's—Associated Actors and Artistes of America. An artist who is a member of one of the unions belonging to the four A's, or a parent union, is entitled to join any or all of the others at a reduced initiation fee (usually half of the regular fee).

Actors' Equity Association (AEA)

The Actor's Equity Association (165 West 46th Street, New York, NY 10036) is a union of actors who work in the theater. Singing actors who work in a musical production usually belong to AEA. Equity negotiates with the producers of Broadway, off-Broadway, regional, summer, and dinner theaters, for working conditions, benefits, and wages. Equity also franchises agents and has its own contract form.

American Federation of Radio
and Television Artists (AFTRA)

AFTRA (260 Madison Avenue, New York, NY 10016) is another labor union. Its membership is made up of performers, actors, announcers, newscasters, sportscasters, and singers who record on video and audiotape or work live in radio and television broadcasting.

AFTRA negotiates with record companies, television and radio networks, jingle producers, and television producers for working conditions, benefits, and wage scales. AFTRA also franchises agents and publishes its own contract form.

American Guild of Musical Artists (AGMA)

AGMA (230 West 55th Street, New York, NY 10019) represents singers and dancers who work as soloists and in chorus for the opera and the ballet, as well as soloists in the concert field.

American Guild of Variety Artists (AGVA)

AGVA (184 Fifth Avenue, New York, NY 10010) represents performers who work in nightclubs, cabarets, resorts, circuses, and in Las Vegas hotel floor shows. A nightclub singer would belong to this union.

Screen Actors Guild (SAG)

The Screen Actors Guild (7065 Hollywood Boulevard, Hollywood, CA 90028) is primarily a film actors' union. However, singers and instrumentalists performing in film (on- or off-camera) also belong to SAG.

SAG negotiates with television and theatrical movie producers for working conditions, benefits, and wages. The guild also franchises agents and publishes its own contract forms.

SGA has offices in Hollywood; New York; Boston; Chicago; Detroit; Dallas; Colorado; Washington, D.C.; San Francisco; Philadelphia; San Diego; Atlanta; Phoenix; Nashville; Houston; and Coral Gables, Florida.

THE SONGWRITERS GUILD OF AMERICA (SGA)

Founded as the Songwriters Protective Association, later changed to American Guild of Authors and Composers (AGAC), and yet again changed to Songwriters Guild, it is today known as the Songwriters Guild of America (SGA). The original name of this organization indicates its function, then and now. However, the guild not only protects, but also represents and educates songwriters. Its more than 5,000 members are composers and lyricists of both serious music and popular music.

The guild publishes a recommended publishing contract that may or may not be used by its members. However, many publishers accept and use this contract form. The guild also represents songwriters in Washington, D.C., and has been instrumental in convincing Congress that the songwriter has valid needs, in terms of legislation and copyright.

The guild audits the books of publishing companies and in the past has recovered millions of dollars in royalties for its songwriter members. The Songwriters Guild of America sponsors seminars that teach the craft and business of songwriting, lyric writing, and jingle writing. It conducts an ASKAPRO session in which members (and nonmembers, for a fee) can listen and ask questions of industry professionals. There is also a song critique session where writers can get professional criticism of their materials.

The organization's newsletter, published four times a year and available to nonmembers, contains much important songwriting news. There is also a collaborator's list available.

Guild offices are located in New York, Nashville, and Los Angeles:

The Songwriters Guild of America
276 Fifth Avenue
New York, NY 10001

6430 Sunset Boulevard
Hollywood, CA 90028

50 Music Square West
Nashville, TN 37203

NASHVILLE SONGWRITERS ASSOCIATION, INTERNATIONAL (NSAI)

The Nashville Songwriters Association, International (1025 16th Avenue South, Nashville, TN 37212) has a membership of over 2,400 songwriters. It has approximately 18 workshops across the United States that have regular meetings where songwriters can discuss their craft and the business of songwriting, and critique each other's work. The association is open to songwriters in all categories of music.

The headquarters is in Nashville. NSAI maintains a list of publishers in the Nashville area. A winter symposium and a summer seminar, open to both members and nonmembers, are held each year in Nashville. NSAI publishes a newsletter four times a year.

NATIONAL ACADEMY OF TELEVISION ARTS AND SCIENCES (NATAS)

The members of NATAS represent all the crafts that produce television programming. They also present the annual Emmy Awards, locally and nationally. The New York chapter (New York Television Academy) publishes a directory listing all its members by category. There is a music section that lists composer, arranger, conductor, instrumentalist, lyricist, music executive, music supervisor, and music producer members. NATAS and the New York Television Academy also publish a newsletter and sponsor an annual Night at the Round Tables Seminar. The seminar features industry professionals on a one-to-one basis, which gives students and young professionals the opportunity to meet with, learn from, and network with these experts. Each seminar always features a music-in-television table.

PERFORMING RIGHTS SOCIETIES

ASCAP, BMI, and SESAC grant licenses to television and radio stations, television and radio networks, hotels, restaurants, clubs, and other users of music. A blanket license allows the user of music to publicly perform any of the copyrighted music in that society's catalog. The user pays the society a fee, which in turn is paid to the publisher and writer members whose music is being used.

American Society of Composers, Authors and Publishers (ASCAP)

The ASCAP Foundation (One Lincoln Plaza, New York, NY 10023) sponsors a series of workshops in New York, Nashville, and Los Angeles. The workshops are for all categories of music (film score, theater, and pop), and they are open to both ASCAP members and nonmembers. ASCAP also gives grants to young composers, as well as scholarships and awards. Major ASCAP offices are located in New York, Nashville, Los Angeles, Puerto Rico, and London, along with 19 branch offices around the country.

Broadcast Music, Inc. (BMI)

BMI (320 West 57th Street, New York, NY 10019) awards cash prizes to composers of serious music who are under the age of 26, in order to help pay for their education. BMI offers a musical theater workshop in New York and sponsors a film scoring workshop in Los Angeles. BMI has offices in New York, Hollywood, London, and three other control offices in the country.

SESAC

SESAC (156 West 56th Street, New York, NY 10019) offers its members legal advice on copyrights, placement assistance with publishers and record companies, and an artist and repertoire consultation. SESAC offices are located in New York City, Nashville, and Los Angeles.

MUSIC PERFORMANCE TRUST FUND (MPTF)

The Music Performance Trust Fund is a nonprofit organization founded in 1948 as a result of an agreement between the Recording Industry of America and the American Federation of Musicians. The group was formed to offset the lack of live musical performances caused by increased use of phonograph records. Its sole purpose was, and is, to present live, admission-free, instrumental musical programs which contribute to the knowledge of and appreciation for music.

MPTF is funded by contributions from record companies based on a percentage of their sales of phonograph records, cassette tapes, and CD's. These monies are used to present thousands of free, live programs every year throughout the United States and Canada. Businesses, schools, government agencies, banks, chambers of commerce, radio stations, hospitals, and other appropriate institutions invest additional monies as cosponsors. This helps make possible many more free, live musical events.

In 1989–1990, more than $8 million was spent to present over 40,000 live and admission-free programs in the United States and Canada, in such places as veteran's hospitals, schools, block parties, nursing homes, shopping malls, and public parks. Whether a fifty-piece orchestra, large band, combo, or single strolling musician, all performances are open to the public with no charge.

A musician wishing to play an MPTF engagement should contact her or his AFM local and register with the local's MPTF Selection Committee. Payment is calculated at the local's prevailing wage, plus pension and welfare benefits.

CHAPTER 6

THE POPULAR PERFORMER: CLUB DATES

Club dates (single engagements) or as they are called in some areas, casuals, can be a good source of income for both full-time and part-time musicians and singers. Club dates are typically parties, weddings, or dinner dances, and they are usually referred to as single engagements. If you're willing to learn the necessary repertoire and perform in the style called for, then you stand a chance of making a living in the club date field.

Club date musicians generally free-lance, working with different musicians on each job, forming what is called a pickup band. Suppose a bandleader books a job for an eight-piece orchestra; the first thing he or she does is hire a subleader to run the job. Then the contractor calls the rest of the musicians and books them for the job. They may have worked together before, or they may be meeting for the first time on that job. The subleader calls out the tunes and tempos, and coordinates and runs the job.

Some bands, on the other hand, are set units. For example, three, four, or five musicians may get together and form a group, rehearsing together to develop a repertoire and style. The trend today is to hire set groups that specialize in the current Top 40 hits of the day. Sometimes a set group is hired and then augmented with free-lance club date musicians to make up a larger band, and also to perform any specialized or ethnic styles of music.

The job can be in a hotel, a restaurant, a catering hall, a private home, a boat, or just anywhere the purchaser of the music wants to have the party. This means portability, and that means equipment and transportation. You must have the equipment needed to perform (electric piano, synthesizer, amplifier, microphone, and speakers) and be able to get it to the job site. With today's instruments that means a station wagon or a van. Jobs are often far away from your home, and you have to allow time for travel, unloading, and setting up the equipment. Some leaders hire roadies (helpers) to unload and set up.

A band is usually booked for four hours; the fifth and sixth hours are usually considered overtime. Some jobs are shorter; for instance, a fashion show or cocktail party can be one, two, or three hours. A job generally runs 55 minutes of playing, and 5 minutes of break time. However, that differs from leader to leader, and from area to area.

ONE PERFORMER'S DAY

If you happen to have a club date in the afternoon, your day could last as long as 16 hours. Suppose the wedding party starts at noon for cocktails and runs from one to five for dinner, dancing, and ceremonies. In order to be set up by noon, you have to leave your house at 10:30, arrive at 11:30, unload and set up, and play from noon to 1:00 in the cocktail area. At 1:00 you move your equipment to the dining area and play from 1:00 to 5:00. The job is then over.

But then you have to rush to break down, load up the equipment, and drive to the next job, which starts at 7:00. You arrive at 6:30, unload, and set up. You play the cocktail party from 7:00 to 8:00, and at 8:00 you move your equipment to the dining area and make music from 8:00 to midnight. At midnight, the host of the party comes over to you and requests that you play an additional hour overtime, so you continue until 1:00 in the morning. At 1:00, you finally break down, load the car, and drive home.

As you fall into bed at 2:30 A.M., you remember that tomorrow is Sunday, and you have another two engagements. That's how it goes, sometimes!

ECONOMICS

For a weekend like the one just described (four club dates), according to the 1990 Local 802 single engagement pay scale, a band member would earn over $600 and the subleader would earn over $900, leaving enough money for the leader to cover business expenses and also make a profit. If the leader were very busy, the musicians could earn additional monies from some midweek work. (Saturday evenings usually pay a premium rate over the weekly scale.)

There is a lot of work in the club date field, but unfortunately there are more musicians than jobs. The constant hustle to stay employed can be very frustrating. There is also a trend to use DJ's instead of live musicians, which also cuts down on the number of jobs available. However, an enterprising leader might be able to sell the client the idea of using a live band (since there is no substitute for live music), combined with a DJ for the prerecorded dance music. That way the guests will have a variety of music and entertainment.

Club dates occur all year, but there is a busy and a slow season. The busy months are May, June, October, November, and December. The other months can be very slow. Some musicians work resorts in the summer months and cruise ships in the winter months. Staying flexible and versatile is one way to survive as a free-lance musician.

WHAT IT TAKES TO BE A CLUB DATE MUSICIAN

Club date musicians must not only have strong backs and lots of stamina, they must also have an endless supply of songs at their fingertips. The repertoire is extremely demanding. You literally are expected to know everything, and the ability to memorize is essential. You are expected to know the music of the 1930s through current hits of the 1990s. Ethnic music, Latin American music, waltzes, specialty numbers, games, even the Star Spangled Banner—the club date musician plays it all.

Sight-reading is not a prerequisite for most club date bands, but it is an asset. The better bands do play for shows, and reading skills are essential. Some bands have a book (band arrangements) and, again, reading music is necessary.

In some orchestras, doubling is required—for example, guitar-bass-vocals, piano-accordion-vocals, sax-flute-clarinets, trumpet-flügelhorn, violin-sax. An ability to play several instruments might get you more jobs.

You have to be able to work well with other musicians and be willing to put your ego and artistic temperament aside. Jazz virtuosity is not needed. Cooperation, attitude, and personality are all very important. Many musicians look at club dates as square music, but working them can buy a lot of square meals.

Musicianship varies from band to band. There are some very mediocre players making a good living in the club date field, but the really fine players are the ones who make the most and are always busy. A leader must have a good personality and a good sense of pacing. Most importantly, a leader must be a diplomat, in order to deal with the different personalities of each client. The pressure of hosting a party sometimes causes people to act strangely. A leader must have a cool head and know how to stay calm and keep the customer smiling.

It is not necessary to belong to a union to work some club dates, but the real professionals are union members, and they play the better jobs. If you work with union professionals, you generally make contacts through them. Most musicians who work club dates free-lance as studio musicians, pit musicians, nightclub performers, and so on. These are the people to know. They generally recommend musicians to each other.

SAMPLE REPERTOIRE

Club date musicians need to develop an extensive repertoire. Cole Porter's "Anything Goes", "From This Moment On", "I Get a Kick Out of You", or "Night and Day" are good choices. George Gershwin's "'S Wonderful'", "But Not for Me", "Love Walked In", and "Nice Work if You Can Get It" are also popular. You should also know many Broadway show tunes and songs from the repertoires of other composers: Jerome Kern, Richard Rodgers, Jimmy Van Heuson, Sammy Cahn, and so on.

In addition to having a large repertoire, you should be familiar with all types of dance beats: two-beat, swing, rumba, waltz, cha-cha, rock and roll, disco, game dances, polka, and ethnic dances.

With all this knowledge, you will be ready for any type of club date: weddings, bar mitzvahs, birthday parties, anniversaries, graduations, dinner dances, fashion shows, retirement parties, engagement parties, beauty pageants, and Christmas parties.

INSTRUMENTAL COMBINATIONS

A club date band is usually composed of a keyboard player (electric piano or synthesizer), a drummer, sax, guitar, trumpet, and sometimes an electric bass. Because of electronic technology, electric pianos, synthesizers, and organs can simulate a bass line, so for small jobs the bass player is usually replaced by the left hand of the keyboard player.

Most trios consist of piano (acoustical), bass, and drums; or electric piano, drums, and guitar or sax.

Most quartets are made up of piano (acoustical), bass, drums, and a guitar, a sax, or a trumpet. Others combine electric piano and/or synthesizer (left hand bass), drums, guitar, and a sax or a trumpet. When more than three horns are used, make sure they can fake; otherwise, it will be necessary to have arrangements.

Big Bands can include these instruments: piano, bass, drums, guitar, three trumpets, three trombones, two alto saxes, two tenor saxes, and a baritone sax. Any combination can be used to suit the sound of your own arrangements.

WHERE TO FIND WORK

Restaurants, dance halls, churches, synagogues, retirement villages, prisons, condominiums, and VFW halls are all potential club date locations. All kinds of organizations hire bands: banks, corporations, labor unions, fraternal and civic groups (like Masons, Rotary Club), foundations, political parties, and hospitals.

HOW TO FIND WORK

Believe it or not, if you look through the help-wanted column of the *New York Times,* you'll find an ad reading: "Musicians and singers wanted for club date work." Sometimes a local newspaper will have an advertisement for musicians and singers. Also, some band leaders advertise in the union papers.

Look in the yellow pages of your telephone book for orchestras. Or walk into a catering establishment and ask, "Who is the bandleader that does your work?" Find out who contracts in your area, and let him or her know that you are available for work. If you are ambitious, inventive, and persistent, you will be noticed and, eventually, you will be playing your first club date. After a while, you may become a club date leader yourself.

Studying with a professional musician who does club dates is another way of learning your way around the business. Try to meet some of the musicians who are working with your teachers, through the union, or for friends. Ask to accompany them to the jobs, help them out with their equipment, and ask questions. You'll learn. Getting into the inner circle is the key to everything. Take notes on the songs that are being played, and be aware of inside tips.

GOING ON THE ROAD

Although club dates are one-nighters, you don't always return home after the show. If it's very far, then you are given accommodations for the night. Working one-nighters with a band or show that travels a concert circuit is very different. A string of one-nighters can keep you on the road for months. That adds up to employment, contacts, and development of your skills.

Only the finest players are selected for road tours. Reading skills are necessary, musicianship is usually of the highest caliber, and the music can be very exciting. Some of these groups are under the baton of famous bandleaders and are put together by contractors or agents.

STEADY ENGAGEMENTS

A steady engagement is a job that is two to six nights a week in the same place. The engagement can last for two weeks, six months, or for years. In the 1940s, large orchestras worked steady engagements in hotels and dance halls. In the 1950s, the smaller jazz and rock combos started working more steadily. Today very few places employ large orchestras or combos for dance music. However, smaller groups and single artists are working quite a bit. There is a recent trend in some hotels to hire harpists, strolling violins, and guitarists, but the pianist is still the most popular choice.

Pianists generally work in cocktail lounges, restaurants, and hotels. Singing piano players dominate the piano bar and saloon circuit. Trio work is rare, but jobs do exist. Playing or singing in restaurants and in cocktail lounges requires a good personality, as well as good musicianship and a well-rounded repertoire. When playing in a restaurant or cocktail lounge, you can expect requests for every song ever written. Knowing the songs that are requested the most, and politely bowing out when you don't know a request, is important.

The better the musician, the better the job. Nightclubs, restaurants, hotels, dance halls, resorts, cruise ships, casinos, piano bars, and saloons are all possible places for steady engagements. If you are inventive, ambitious, and a good salesperson, perhaps you can create a job. In fact, there is a bank on the east side of

Manhattan that features a woman pianist performing every day of the week.

Steady work is generally rather intimate, and a lot of personal contact with the audience is necessary, so you must enjoy meeting and talking with people. Everybody loves an entertainer, and you'll find yourself on a first-name basis with all the customers. That's a beginning for you, and it's how you build a following. Keep a list of the people who come into the club frequently, and remember their requests. A following (or mailing list) is very important to your career.

A steady engagement can consist of middle-of-the-road music (a little bit of everything), jazz, country, Top 40 (current hits), standards, rock, Dixieland, and many other styles of music. The music can be for dancing or listening, soft and subdued, or loud and exciting. It all depends on the situation. Keeping up with current trends is very important. For instance, nostalgia is very big today. There is still a following for the Big Band sounds of the 1940s and the rock and roll sounds of the 1950s.

Look through the entertainment section of your local paper. Make a list of all the clubs and restaurants that have live music. Make the rounds, and introduce yourself to the owners and managers.

It is not necessary to belong to the union for some of the smaller jobs, but as you upgrade your career and start working in the better rooms, you will be well served by belonging to the union. You must get work in order to gain experience and get exposure, and, of course, your second job will never happen if you don't get your first.

Pay Scale

A steady gig can pay $75 per night, or it can pay $200 per night. It all depends on the club. Is it union or nonunion, small or large?

Is it your first job, or are you an established act? 1990 Local 802 pay scale for a New York City hotel was $598.94 a week (five hours a night, five nights a week) for a band member. That kind of work is nice if you can get it, but most hotel musicians stay forever, and openings are rare.

According to the same pay scale, hotels paid $748.68 for a solo pianist (five hours, five nights). However, a restaurant right across the street may pay less, or more, depending on the act. There are many unscrupulous agents and club owners who take advantage of the overcrowded profession by paying substandard salaries.

Sometimes you get what you can according to your talent, your reputation, and the following you've achieved. A union job will also give you some benefits, such as pension, health, and vacation.

A leader, or a soloist, receives more money according to the size of the group. Pay is calculated as scale plus an additional percentage; the more band members, the higher that percentage. Here are some examples:

- Scale + 25% (for a single musician) = $748.68.
- Scale + 50% (for two musicians) = $894.41 for the bandleader, $598.94 for band members.
- Scale + 75% (for 3–6 musicians) = $1048.15 for the bandleader, $598.94 for band members.
- Scale + 100% (for 7 or more musicians) = $1197.88 for the bandleader, $590.94 for band members.

These figures are based on Local 802, 1990 pay scale, five hours per night, five nights per week; different locals have different wage scales. Engagements also have different scales depending on how many hours the musicians play. (Note: a musician who doubles as a singer is entitled to an additional 10 percent premium.)

Resorts

A resort hotel is a small vacation city, and like a city it has restaurants, nightclubs, and cocktail lounges. Wherever they are, resorts have music and entertainment. Most of them have an entertainment director who works with an agent.

A simple telephone call to the music and entertainment director can provide answers to all your questions. Find out if he or she keeps files and who the agent is who books the music and entertainment. You may need to send a picture and resume, as well as a demonstration tape and a press kit. You may get called for an audition, so have something ready.

The entertainment varies from resort to resort. Some have large bands, while others have small bands. Some have full-time and others have part-time entertainment. Many resorts book name entertainers, and the band is required to play the show. That means reading skills are essential. Singer/pianist and self-contained lounge groups are used quite often.

To secure either part-time or full-time work, you have to do your homework. The pay scales vary at the resorts and usually include room and board.

Cruise Ships

Ever since the hit TV series "Love Boat" was launched, the cruise ship industry has been experiencing a boom. More and more cruises are leaving for exotic South Seas islands and around-the-world-in-80-days voyages. Since ships are floating resorts, it stands to reason that they have their share of restaurants, cocktail lounges, nightclubs, and piano bars. They even have small theaters. Recently, *Backstage* published a list of cruise ship lines, along with the agents, entertainment directors, and producers who hire the musicians, singers, dancers, and actors. One company produces small-scale versions of Broadway musicals. Another produces Las Vegas–type shows. Cruise ship musicians must be able to play dance music, play for shows, and mingle with the guests. They must have good personalities and enjoy meeting and talking with people.

Cruise ships sail from New York, Los Angeles, Florida, San Francisco, and Texas. You can find their addresses by looking through travel magazines or the travel section of the newspaper. Call a cruise ship line and find out if they keep their own entertainment files, if you can audition, or who the agent or producer is who books the music and entertainment.

Some musicians and entertainers are booked for long periods of time (three or six months). Some musicians make cruise work their career and stay on board for years. Salaries vary and, of course, include room and board. You are on call seven days a week and on the ship 24 hours a day. One big advantage of working a cruise ship is that you get to see the whole world, so if you like to travel, and get paid at the same time, then the open sea may be for you.

The Backstage Handbook for Performing Artists has a list of cruise ship lines, agents, and producers. Here is a partial list of some cruise ship lines:

Holland America Cruises, New York
Princess Cruises, Los Angeles
Royal Viking Line, San Francisco
Scandinavian World Cruises, Miami
Cunard Lines, England
Costa Line, Miami
Easter Cruises, Miami
Paquet Lines, Miami
Carnival Cruises, Miami

NIGHTCLUB SINGERS

A nightclub singer is someone who sings in a nightclub and performs what is called a floor show. A singer who does a floor show, or a stand-up act, is either the headliner or the opening act. The opening act is sometimes referred to as a stand-up singer.

Generally, if a comedian is the star of the show, a singer is booked as the opening act. And if a singer is the star, then a comedian is the opening act. If it's a really big show, there might be a dance team, a chorus line with a production singer, or even a magic act.

Someone starting a career as a nightclub singer should work with a vocal coach who is familiar with the repertoire and style of nightclubs and cabarets. The singer should begin with lead sheets of the songs he or she wants to use in the act. That way songs can be tried in a showcase situation, before spending money on arrangements. After enough songs have been broken in, and their keys and arrangements set, they can then be transposed into piano/vocal parts or made into arrangements. To a singer, songs are like tailor made clothes, and they must fit perfectly.

If a singer has a lot of money to spend on a show, then someone called an act builder is hired. (Sometimes the arranger will also help build the act.) The act builder creates the entire show: selection of songs, arrangements, staging, microphone technique, choreography, patter (dialogue with the audience), wardrobe, sound, and lighting. In most cases, the act builder works with the pianist/accompanist, who may also be the arranger/orchestrator/conductor. Some singers work only with their own conductors, who may also play the piano while conducting the show.

In most cases, a singer gets a rehearsal, but since rehearsals can be expensive and time-consuming, a singer must be prepared to do a talk-over. The musicians and the leader read their charts (music) as the singer talks them through the act. A singer must be very familiar with the arrangements and know how to explain them to the musicians.

An act usually runs from 30 minutes to one hour, depending on the show. Some clubs want two different shows a night, and that could mean 8 to 17 songs per show and 16 to 34 arrangements. Some singers carry as many as 50 arrangements with them.

Although the singer's act may be set, new songs should constantly be added to keep it fresh. It's a big investment for a singer: between the act builder, choreographer, arranger, copying costs, and wardrobe, the costs could add up to thousands of dollars. Some singers have their own wireless microphones and carry their own sound systems. Before singers invest a lot of hard-earned money into an act, they should be sure they have the voice, stage presence, charisma, and personality to command center stage.

It's not easy standing on stage all alone between an orchestra and an audience. It takes a lot of energy and talent to be dynamic and exciting. A singer not only needs a good voice, but must also move well. An ability to dance can be readily incorporated into the act. Many singers also have a flair for comedy, although they should be careful not to upstage any comedians who are on the bill.

A show can pay $300, or it can pay several thousand dollars; it all depends on your talent, your act, your personality, your ability to perform, and, of course, your stature in the business.

Singers work everywhere, from nightclubs to theme parks, with Big Bands, small bands, and in studios. The work can be seasonal and, in most cases, requires a lot of travel.

A good how-to reference for actors, singers, and dancers is *Backstage Handbook for Performing Artists* by Sherry Eaker (Backstage Publications Inc., 330 West 42nd Street, New York, NY 10036).

JAZZ

The market for jazz singers and instrumentalists is very limited. Although the musicianship is very high, the monetary rewards are very low, unless you have a hit record. Most jazz players have to play commercial music—shows, club dates, teaching, and studio work—in order to survive. American jazz is very popular in Europe and Japan, and many jazz artists travel abroad and make a living performing outside the United States.

Many jazz recording artists have combined their music with the dance rhythms of reggae, rock, disco, and Latin to get themselves onto the charts and into the concert circuit. For example, in 1970, the legendary Miles Davis won a Grammy Award for his innovative fusion album *Bitches Brew*. The album featured jazz pianist Chick Corea, who has been successful fusing jazz and Latin. Herbie Hancock's work with electronic instruments and disco dance rhythms scored him a number one hit called "Rockit." Jazz guitarist George Benson has added the sound of his singing with the sound of plush string arrangements, fusing jazz, rhythm and blues, and pop, for a successful middle-of-the-road (MOR) sound. And more recently the jazz saxophonist David Sanborn became a top-selling fusion artist.

However, classical trumpeter Wynton Marsalis, at the age of 21, won two Grammys in 1983: one for Best Solo Jazz Instrumentalist and one for Best Classical Instrumentalist. He has gone on to win six more since then, as well as to score a feature film. Marsalis has begun a renaissance in jazz, and his influence has opened doors for many young players using acoustical instruments, creating a whole new market for traditional jazz. In fact the outlook for jazz is far healthier than it has been in decades.

Harry Connick, Jr., who just celebrated his twenty-third birthday in 1990, started out as a jazz pianist then crossed over to the

Big Band sound and the Sinatra style of singing that has put him onto the charts and into the star category.

Organizations

Many organizations offer information, money, and assistance to jazz artists. The National Endowment for the Arts has a jazz program that awards grants to jazz composers and performers. The Jazz World Society (P.O. Box 777, Times Square Station, New York, NY 10108-0777) maintains a data base of information related to jazz. The International Association of Jazz Educators (NAJE) (P.O. Box 724, Manhattan, KS 66502) publishes a list of schools that offer degrees in jazz. The association is active in promoting the study and appreciation of jazz. It also publishes a journal and a newsletter.

Jazzmobile, Inc. was founded in 1964 by jazz pianist/composer/educator Dr. Billy Taylor to instruct, present, propagate, and preserve jazz, "America's classical music," as a national treasure. Jazzmobile produces concerts, festivals, and special events on a worldwide basis. Their address is: Jazzmobile, 154 West 127th Street, New York, NY 10027.

The National Jazz Service Organization exists to nurture the growth and enhancement of jazz music as an American art form by providing information and services to individuals and organizations committed to the creation, performance, instruction, presentation, and preservation of jazz music. The organization has a technical assistance program in such areas as jazz marketing, demo tape evaluation, grant writing, career development, and touring. They also publish a quarterly journal. Their address is: National Jazz Service Organization, P.O. Box 50152, Washington, DC 20004-0152.

CHAPTER 7

THE RECORDING INDUSTRY

The record company is where all the action is. The company produces and promotes the artist, distributes and sells the product, and collects and pays the money.

Record companies are corporations and therefore require the skills and talents of a large variety of professionals. Some companies are more on the creative side, while others are more corporate. Creative record companies are usually run by music people—musicians, arrangers, and producers who are very involved with producing the records and developing the artists. More corporate-structured companies are run by lawyers and accountants, and depend on independent producers to record and develop the artists. However, the current trend for corporate companies is to have more executives with music backgrounds. The "Big Six"—CBS, RCA, Warner, IEM/Capitol, Polygram, and MCA—are large corporate record companies. Smaller companies like A&M, Arista, and Geffen tend to be creatively oriented. Recently, Sony Corporation purchased CBS Records, Polygram purchased A&M, and MCA purchased Geffen Records.

There are over two thousand record companies listed in Billboard's 1990 *International Buyers Guide* and approximately seven thousand recording artists listed in Billboard's *Talent and*

Touring Directory. Many labels specialize in one or two categories, with a minimum number of artists, while the larger companies maintain a large number of artists in many categories. In fact, CBS Records has a roster of approximately two hundred artists in all categories, while RCA has about a hundred.

Depending on the status of the artist, the company will either assign a producer (on-staff or independent), or the artist will choose the producer. Many superstars have their own publishing companies and demand to own all or part of the publishing rights of their songs.

The record industry is big business, with records selling in the millions and total sales in the billions. According to a report by the Recording Industry Association of America (RIAA), an all-time high number of units shipped in 1989. The dollar volume for the year was $6.46 billion, which is 3.35 percent over the dollar volume in 1988, which was $6.25 billion. This continued steady growth reflects a healthy industry.

A 1988 RIAA Statistical Overview shows the following breakdown of dollars spent on different types of music:

Rock 46.2%
Pop 15.2%
Black/Urban 13.3%
Country 7.4%
Gospel 2.5%
Classical 3.5%
Jazz 4.7%
Other 6%

THE MAKING OF A RECORD

It takes a record company and its whole staff to plan and coordinate the strategy necessary to sell a record. The artist and repertoire (A&R) department is headed by the vice-president of A&R, who may also be a staff producer responsible for the productions of some of the major artists with the label. Under the vice-president is the staff A&R producer, who is responsible for recording and producing albums and singles with assigned artists. The A&R department prepares budgets and handles the paperwork both for the department and for the recording sessions.

The director of the talent acquisitions department could also be considered a talent scout. It is that department's responsibility to find new artists, produce demos, and participate in the selection and signing of artists. The people who work in both of these departments must have a good ear and a feel for commercial songs and artists. They must be completely familiar with the music ratings charts and be tuned in to the styles and trends of the music world.

The artist, having been discovered by the director of talent acquisition and brought into the company with the approval of the entire A&R staff and its director, is then ready to begin planning the album. The A&R director, along with the producer (and possibly the artist's manager), plans the concept of the album and selects the songs. If the artist is also a songwriter, then some of her or his songs may be used.

The artist is given a budget, which is used to plan the number of musicians, arrangements, and studio time. The A&R manager then coordinates the session with the studio manager or traffic manager of the recording studio. For many years, record companies maintained their own in-house recording studios, but they have discontinued this practice and now use independent, outside studios for their recordings.

After the session is finished (recorded and mixed), the master is sent to the plant to be readied for production. The original tapes are carefully filed away by the vault manager.

Meanwhile, back at the record company, the creative services department has been very busy. The vice-president of creative services plans the budget and administers the advertising, art, publicity, and packaging. The advertising manager plans the advertising campaign and, according to the amount of exposure planned, selects the appropriate media. The media buyer then coordinates the advertising campaign with radio, television, trade magazines, and newspapers.

The art director supervises the project and assigns the work to the photographers, graphic artists, designers, and copywriters, who together prepare the album cover and the ad layouts. The camera-ready art work is sent to the printers and turned into album covers, cassette and CD covers, and inserts; these are shipped to the manufacturing plant and, together with the LP pressing, the CD and the cassette tape, are assembled into the final product. While all this recording and drawing, printing and pressing is going on, the product manager, the A&R department, and the artist's manager plan all the strategies involved with releasing the album. They coordinate the release date with the directors of promotion, marketing, public relations, and sales.

The director of artist development, along with the artist's manager and concert promoter, plan the live performances, the promotion tour, radio and television appearances, special concerts, and everything else that will make the public aware of the artist and the record. A record that doesn't get heard doesn't get sold, and the function of the promotion department is to make sure that the record gets on the air. The vice-president of promotion is in charge of the directors of national promotion, regional promotion, and local promotion. Promotion personnel go into the field and work with radio station promotion directors and DJ's on both the secondary stations and the major stations for airplay. The promotion people in the field build relationships with the local disc jockeys and record stores. They stimulate interest in the artist and report sales to the radio stations and to the tip sheets (a special trade paper that goes out to radio stations). They report all action to the trade papers, such as *Billboard* and *Variety*.

An artist's promotion tour usually includes a guest appearance on the local DJ's radio show, the local television show, and an appearance at the local record store to sign autographs; all of this is planned and coordinated by the promotion department. The director of press information, the publicist, and the director of marketing all work at securing press coverage and exposure.

Sales managers, merchandising managers, and distribution managers all work towards one end: to get the record to the consumer. Large record companies work with many college promotion and/or marketing departments, and have a "college rep." He or she acts as an intern and is responsible for getting airplay on the college radio station and putting up posters that advertise the artist and the record.

The copyright administrator deals with publishers in matters of licenses, royalties, and copyrights. The vice-president of business affairs negotiates with artists' managers, producers, and publishers. A musician with education or experience in sales, marketing, management, or business administration could get a good start in the music business with a record company. Record companies like to promote from within, as well as hire from within the field, and a job opening for a trainee might just be the start of a music career.

Record companies are all over the country, but the main concentration of companies is in New York, Nashville, and Los Angeles. The large companies have offices in all three cities, as well as small offices all around the country. These small offices operate much like the main office, and a job with a small office can lead to the main office.

There is very little turnover in the business, but there are job opportunities at the lower levels as well as the executive levels. Openings are sometimes advertised in the help-wanted ads in newspapers and in the trade magazines. Also, there are employment agencies that specialize in record and publishing company jobs. Trade papers that dispense music business information are *Billboard, Cashbox,* and *Variety.*

RECORDING ARTISTS

The ultimate goal of nearly every musician and singer is to be a recording artist. The prestige of having a record and the exposure from TV, radio, and magazine promotion can improve the quality of bookings and attract the attention of agents and managers who can further an artist's career. A hit record can skyrocket an artist from total obscurity to international fame in a very short time. Getting a recording contract, however, is no easy matter, and getting a hit is almost impossible. Even a hit record has to be backed up with a dynamite act, a good video, a second, and even a third hit, in order to solidify the performer's career as a recording artist.

As a performing artist, you can approach talent scouts with a demo, by knocking on their doors or through lawyers, managers, producers, or other artists who have gained the confidence of talent scouts. Talent scouts often travel to many cities to listen to an artist that a local promoter or disc jockey recommended. Live performance is extremely important in getting a record company interested in signing you, and in addition to sounding good, an artist must also look good.

Building a following and generating a lot of excitement can influence a record executive just as it can an audience. That's what the executive is looking for, an artist who can deliver on the promotion tour and sell records. The average life span of an unprepared artist is five years. That is why it is important to take the time to develop good performing skills by studying, practicing, and working in clubs.

MAKING THE DEMO

Before you make a demo, you should know exactly what you want it to show. For example, if your focus is the song, it takes one kind of demo, if it's the singing, the band, or the production, that takes another. Is it a song that requires a heavy drum beat, or one that shows off the lyrics, the melody, or the arrangement? All of these factors must be considered and the session carefully planned before spending hard earned money on a record date. If you have a unique, original, and exciting sound in a live performance, then that is what you have to capture in the studio. That's what makes a performer a recording artist. The demo, or demomaster, should sound as professional as possible so that the recording company will know exactly what you sound like on record. You are the best judge of your sound by comparing the demo to the records already on the charts. If you show some promise of becoming a hit act, you might be able to make a deal with a studio owner. Many recording artists have received free studio time in exchange for a piece of the action. You might even produce yourself with your own money or with backers' money.

Once you have a finished master, you can approach the record companies with it. Some labels are willing to listen to a finished master rather than just a demo. If a company signs an artist on the strength of a demo, then they first have to start planning the album. However, a self-contained performer who writes his or her own songs, and has a finished master, may be more desirable to a record company.

PRODUCERS

The producer is the person responsible for making the record. Some record companies have staff producers, and others contract the services of independent producers. An unknown artist signed to a record contract would be assigned to a producer who would plan the album. However, the superstars have the advantage of choosing who will produce and what songs will be performed.

The 7″-45 RPM single is being phased out, and the single cassette is taking its place. However, today's record business is completely album oriented, and the album as we once knew it (12″ vinyl pressing) is also becoming obsolete and is being replaced by the cassette tape and the CD. Besides the better quality of sound on the CD, it can hold up to 77 minutes of music, as opposed to the LP which holds up to 43 minutes of music on both sides.

From 1983 to 1989, CD sales increased from .8 million units to 207.2 million units. Cassette singles have conquered the singles market, and cassette album sales have risen, while LP's continue to decline.

At one time, a recording artist only had to come up with an "A" side and a "B" side (45 RPM 7″ single). Now that same artist has to come up with 10 to 12 songs to fill an album. Instead of producing two songs (one per each side), a producer has to come out with 10 to 12 songs. And with the competition today, each cut has to be a gem. That means 10 to 12 arrangements, more studio and mixing time, more musicians, more tape, and a lot more money.

A record producer is responsible for the production from start to finish, from the concept to the final mix, from the album cover to the promotion, and from the pressing to the airplay. A producer must know the business and the creative side of music, have a good feel for what is commercial, have an understanding and love for music, and be willing to take chances. He or she must know how to budget a record date, deal with lawyers, contracts, publishers, record company executives, musicians, singers, songwriters, arrangers, engineers, managers, union regulations and, most of all, artistic temperament.

Producers generally start out as engineers, composers, arrangers, studio musicians, artists or professional managers, and they get their training on the job. Sometimes producers will use their own money, the record company's money, the artist's money, or an investor's money to produce an album.

Producers generally earn a royalty on the record sales, and their initial fee can range from $5,000 to $40,000 or more, per album, plus points, usually 2 to 4 percent. The exact fee depends on the type of artist produced and the status of the producer. The producer's fee is generally part of the whole production budget. Many independent producers also own their own publishing companies and earn additional money by including songs from their catalogs on the albums.

Album costs are extremely high, and the following is just a rough estimate of the kind of money it takes to produce and promote an artist today. A rock group can cost $150,000 and up to produce. An established star can range from $250,000 and up. However, production costs for a jazz artist's album can range from $25,000 to $85,000. Promotion costs usually range from $25,000 to $100,000 and more, not including graphics and manufacturing costs.

Then comes the music video. The minimum cost to produce a music video for a new band is $50,000. The more established artists' budgets can be $150,000 and up, and the superstars spend $200,000 and more for their music videos. The music video has become an important asset to promoting an artist and his or her record. In fact, in the early 1980s, the record industry was experiencing a recession, when along came MTV (Music Television). MTV immediately recaptured the interest of young audiences, and record sales began to rise. In some instances the visual is stronger than the music, and the video can create the hit. However, Music Television is reluctant to try a new recording artist; they prefer to play the videos of more established artists. A producer and a record company must have a lot of confidence in an artist before they start spending money on a video.

ENGINEERS

A recording studio is divided into two areas. The studio is where the singers and musicians work. The other area is the control room. The two areas are separated by double plate glass windows, so that both sides can see each other, but no sound will penetrate. Communication is done through microphones and speakers. The studio is acoustically designed (angled walls and ceiling) so that certain frequencies do not cancel each other out, and certain areas are padded with sound-absorbing materials to prevent reverberation and penetration of sound from outside the studio.

The control room is where the console (mixing board), tape decks, and other sophisticated recording equipment are located. The control room is operated by two engineers: one who operates console and works directly under the producer, and one who operates the tape machines. Also on hand is a maintenance engineer whose responsibility it is to repair equipment in the event of a malfunction. The engineers set up the microphones, the musicians, and the baffles (devices that regulate the flow of sound). The engineers are usually assisted by a helper who sets up music stands, chairs, and headphones; plugs in cables; and goes for coffee. This helper is sometimes called a ''go-fer.''

The sound engineer must know how to translate the producer's ideas into buttons, dials, and switches in order to produce the quality of sound desired. Sometimes a recording session will last for many hours, and an engineer must have a lot of patience and stamina. An engineer must be able to work quickly and accurately under pressure, and since studio time is expensive, there is little room for errors. Imagine accidentally erasing a portion of a tape that took hours to record (after the orchestra has already left the studio). It can, and has, happened, and it is a very expensive mistake.

There are many schools and seminars that teach recording techniques. The July 1990 issue of *MIX* magazine published a list of schools. Back issues are available from *MIX* Magazine, 6400 Hollis Street, Suite 12, Emeryville, CA 94608, 1-800-233-9604. *Keyboard Magazine* also has advertisements listing recording schools.

An engineer with a music background can be a valuable asset to a producer of popular or classical music recording sessions. Engineers work on staff as well as free-lance. Salaries can range from $15,000 to $80,000 or more a year, depending upon location and status in the profession. Most engineers, and assistants, usually put in a lot of overtime when working on a project. The high cost of maintaining a studio (rent, staff, and maintenance) has caused many major record companies to close their in-house studios.

The availability of quality multitrack home recording equipment coupled with a computer, MIDI, and a bunch of synthesizers and samplers has made it possible for songwriters, singers, and musicians to do their productions in their home studios. This has taken a lot of work away from the smaller independent studios. However, new digital technology has created the compact disc, or CD, and with it, a healthy outlook for the future. Where there's new technology, there are new opportunities.

The CD is a 4-3/4″ disk digitally encoded with billions of pits that represent up to 77 minutes of music on one side only. These pits are read by a laser beam stylus, then converted back into an analog signal which is fed into a conventional amplifier and speakers to reproduce the recorded sound. However, that's where the difference is: the sound is pure, with no hiss or flutter. With a CD, there's no surface noise, pops, clicks, or interference from dust, scratches, or skipping.

As more consumers purchase CD players, more and more albums will have to be made available. Record producers and engineers will have to learn the new techniques for digital recording. Many recording studios use DAT (digital audiotape) multitrack recording machines, and then mix down to a DAT two-track stereo machine, a new technology that has to be learned. Many studios use automated mixing boards, and an engineer must know how to program the computer for this technology.

PROFESSIONAL ORGANIZATIONS

New Music Seminar
632 Broadway
New York, NY 10012

The New Music Seminar is a five-day convention that's held in New York City each year in July. It covers all aspects of the music industry and is a great educational and networking opportunity. National and international representatives and experts from record companies, publishing companies, booking agencies, and just about every other facet of the industry sit on panels and discuss the business of music. All styles of music are represented, from rock to pop to rap to jazz to film score. Topics include college radio, careers in music, videos, and much, much more. Write to the NMS for information and a brochure.

The Audio Engineers Society, Inc.
(AES)
60 East 42nd Street
New York, NY 10165

The AES is devoted exclusively to audio technology, and its membership is made up of engineers, scientists, administrators, and technicians who deal with audio engineering and acoustics. The society holds conventions and seminars, and publishes a journal which keeps its membership informed about new techniques and equipment.

The National Academy of Recording Arts and Sciences
(NARAS)
303 North Glenoaks Boulevard
Suite 140
Burbank, CA 91502-1178

NARAS membership is made up of singers, musicians, producers, engineers, songwriters, composers, arrangers, and all the other craft people who are involved in the creative process of making records. Chapters are in Los Angeles, New York, Nashville, Chicago, Atlanta, San Francisco, and Memphis.

NARAS presents the annual Grammy Awards, and its members nominate and vote for the winners. NARAS offers seminars, scholarships, a newsletter, a journal, and specially priced, newly released albums, CDs, and tapes.

Write to the national office for the chapter near you.

Society of Motion Picture and Television Engineers
(SMPTE)
595 West Hartsdale Avenue
White Plains, NY 10607

The membership of SMPTE is made up of professionals who work in the motion picture and television industry in the United States, Canada, and 60 other countries. They include engineers, technicians, producers, directors, people in sound recording, and all the other crafts that go into the business of film and video. SMPTE publishes a journal, a newsletter, and books, as well as sponsoring an annual technical conference.

STUDIO SINGERS

Studio singers are also recording artists. They are heard as background vocalists on records, tapes, CDs, film and television, or as group singers and soloists in commercials and jingles. The very successful singers make a lot of money, but it's a competitive field, and very few people do the bulk of the work. A singer who is being used for his or her special sound can become very popular and get a lot of work; however, overexposure can burn someone out.

Producers and ad agencies cast a voice in the same manner that a casting director chooses an actor for a part. When a product is to be advertised for a certain market, they use a singer with the sound that will best represent their product in that market. For example, if a client wants to sell the product in an R&B market, then a singer with an R&B style and sound will be used.

However, a studio singer is a singer first and must have excellent sight-singing skills and knowledge of all musical styles, from classical to gospel. A studio singer must also have a good personality, work well with other singers, and be able to take direction. Most importantly, he or she must be a quick learner. It is also important to have a voice that records well, but even more important is the ability to blend well with other singers. Group singers go on and on. A good ear, good pitch and intonation, good microphone technique, and a good sense of rhythm, along with a wide range, flexibility, and a unique sound are important assets.

Advertising agency music directors, independent producers and contractors usually use the same singers over and over again; however, they do keep demo tapes on file. Occasionally a producer will be looking for a unique or different sound, and a singer who is in the right place at the right time can be discovered! Ideally, a demo tape should contain real on-air commercials. Since a beginner does not have a track record, this is not possible. An alternative is to make up a demo tape from some of your best recorded performances, showing a good variety of your style, range, and flexibility, possibly adding some short spots to show the sound of your voice doing jingles.

A singer with access to a small multitrack MIDI studio could very well put together a demo. There are some studios with access to the actual music tracks of a commercial, without the voice. For a fee, they will over-dub you as the singer and put together a demo tape. Two types of tapes are used: 5″ reel-to-reel and cassette. The cassette seems to be more popular.

At a seminar on jingle singing presented by AFTRA for its membership, the topic "the job market" was addressed by one of New York's top studio singers. Everyone had pad and pen ready to copy down a list of contacts, so that the next day they could be out cutting jingles. The speaker stood up and said, "The job market is wherever you can find it." How true that is. There are no ads or agents for studio work, so it takes determination, motivation, and being in the right place at the right time.

The telephone directory, *The Madison Avenue Handbook, Backstage, TV Film & Tape Production Directory,* and the *Black Book* (a very expensive set of books on the advertising industry) contain lists of advertising agencies and music commercial producers (sometimes called music houses). Making the rounds of these offices is the best way to introduce yourself. However, unless you've been recommended by someone close to the producer, you can expect to be turned away on your first visit. A lot of persistence and self-confidence are needed to show your enthusiasm, so that sooner or later you will be given an opportunity to show your stuff.

Studying voice or sight-singing with a teacher who does studio work, or who has contacts with a producer or a vocal contractor, might help. Belonging to professional organizations made up of singers and/or songwriters is another way to meet the people who may help you to be in the "right place, at the right time."

Singing in a nightclub or musical theater is a good showcase. Inviting music directors, contractors, and producers to see your performance is bringing the right people to the right place. Even if they don't show up, at least they will become familiar with your name and know that you are a working professional.

Recording demos for songwriters and publishers and singing back-up vocals plays a very important part in becoming known in the business. Working among professionals who are studio musicians and singers will bring leads, tips, and introductions. Breaking into studio work is a full-time occupation. In most cases, as mentioned earlier, sight-singing skills are essential, and if sight-singing is not one of your strong points, then start studying, preferably with a professional studio singer who can also guide your career.

AFTRA's 1990 national pay scale for studio singers was $142.00 each for a soloist or duo. For groups of 3 to 5 singers, $157.05 each; for 6 to 8 singers, $139.00 each; and for 9 or more, $123.40 each per session. A session is 1 1/2 hours in which one spot up to 90 seconds can be recorded. Each additional spot is considered a session. The residuals (payment for reruns) are based on how the commercials are aired (television, radio; national, regional, or local) and how many times they are aired. A top studio singer can earn a yearly salary into the six figures. Studio singers belong to the American Federation of Television and Radio Artists (AFTRA) and the Screen Actors Guild (SAG). Studio singers can work wherever there is a studio, and that can be anywhere in the country; however, the main concentration of work is in New York, Chicago, Los Angeles, and Nashville.

Publications that contain a list of ad agencies and music producers (music houses) are: *Madison Avenue Handbook,* Peter Glen Publications, 17 East 48th Street, New York, NY 10017, and *Backstage TV Film & Tape Production Directory,* Backstage Publications, 330 West 42nd Street, New York, NY 10036.

STUDIO MUSICIANS

Studio musicians are recording artists too. Their special and unique talents are heard on records, commercials, jingles, in film, television, and in background music. Many of the studio musicians got their start by doing demos, being part of a famous entertainer's back-up band, playing in a Broadway pit orchestra, being radio or television staff musicians, or by having been recording artists themselves.

A studio musician must have excellent playing and reading skills. Excessive mistakes are not tolerated. He or she must have a special and unique sound that a producer needs. The horns and string players are always reading parts (music). And even though the rhythm players have parts to read, they are sometimes hired for their "feel" for the type of music being recorded. In Nashville, the session players use what is called the Nashville numbers system. It simply means that the chords are called by their numbers and not their names. For example, C, A minor, D minor, and G7 will look like this: 1, 6, 2, 5. *The Nashville Numbers System,* by Arthur D. Levine, explains the system well.

Studio work is booked by contractors. Usually one contractor will book the whole session; however, on larger sessions a second contractor may be hired to book the string players, and a third contractor may book the singers. Producers and composers have their favorite players and generally know who can deliver a special sound that may be needed; they will ask the contractor to book a certain musician or singer for a particular record, jingle, or film sound track.

Studio musicians have to be very flexible and able to play many different styles, as well as double on other instruments in the same family. Patience, a good personality, a positive attitude, and the ability to work well with other musicians is very important. A studio musician must also be able to take direction, and the really good ones are able to contribute ideas and musical suggestions to the producer.

Musicians belong to a local of the American Federation of Musicians of the United States and Canada (AFM). The national pay scale for a basic regular session is $227.57 for three hours in which no more than 15 minutes of music are recorded. Leaders and contractors get double scale. There is also a special session scale of $150.20 for 1 1/2 hours in which no more than 7 1/2 minutes of music can be recorded. A one-hour jingle session will pay $84.30 with 2 to 4 musicians, and $78.00 with 5 or more musicians, for no more than three national spots and a total of three minutes of music to be recorded. Film, television, radio, and TV commercials and recordings all have a different pay scale. Symphonic recording also has a different pay scale. Some musicians, who have a special or unique sound and are in demand, are usually paid double scale and sometimes more. (This extra pay is referred to as overscale.)

Economics and cutbacks can reduce the amount of work available in the recording studio. Electronic synthesizers and samplers have replaced the need for drummers, string players, and horn players for certain sessions. Some producers record the rhythm tracks in this country and go to Europe to record the strings and horns. For the price of an airplane ticket and a hotel, they can save thousands of dollars on the musicians.

Some pianists have become keyboard players; they specialize in programing and performing on synthesizer and samplers (also called programmers). Drummers, too, have learned to work on electronic drums, sequencers, and drum machines. A musician who is employed to play an electronic musical device on a multi-tracking session receives an hourly rate of approximately $200.

The National Association of Recording Arts and Sciences (NARAS) has what is called an MVP Award (most valuable player). The New York chapter sends out a ballot and with it a list of currently active studio musicians. There are approximately 14,000 dues-paying members in New York's Local 802, and approximately 3,000 are active full-time or part-time musicians. The 1988 NARAS list contains the names of 326 musicians and 113 back-up singers, which means that approximately 10 percent of the working professionals in the New York area are considered studio musicians. Some musicians, who also compose, arrange, orchestrate, and produce, start their own production companies. Or, they work as music directors for an advertising agency, as A&R directors with record companies, or as professional managers for a publishing company.

The main concentration of activity for studio musicians is in New York, Nashville, Los Angeles, and Chicago. Other areas like Toronto, Shreveport, Muscle Shoals, Atlanta, Miami, and Memphis also have their share of studio work. Although each area has a variety of work, New York and Chicago have more jingle-recording sessions. Nashville has more country and pop recording sessions, Los Angeles has more feature film and television recording sessions.

CHAPTER 8

MORE MUSIC CAREERS

TEACHING

Music education is a two-sided coin: it is a subject to be learned for its own sake (theory, singing, and instruments) and it is a tool for learning. Studies have shown that young children who participate in music training have a definite advantage over those who don't. Academically, they achieve higher grades in math, reading, and writing; they are good listeners and have a better capacity for comprehension. Music students develop a higher degree of confidence, imagination, and creativity than those who don't study music. Clearly, music is an important basic component in the development and training of children.

Being taught rhythms, melody, music appreciation, and group performance allows students to develop awareness and insights into themselves and the world around them. However, budget cutbacks in recent years have limited the opportunities in music education in the public schools. With all the research and statistics showing the importance of music education, it is still not considered a basic.

A music teacher is a teacher first and should have a degree in education. Some teachers are hired from the field, but with the tight job market, the more education you have, the better chance you'll have of getting a position.

Elementary School Training

According to the Bureau of Labor Statistics, in 1988, 1.4 million teachers worked in kindergarten and elementary schools, and the job opportunities are expected to fluctuate in the early 1990s and increase from the mid-1990s to the year 2000.

Elementary schoolteachers must have a bachelor's degree from an institution with an approved teacher education program. They must also be certified by the state. Information on certification requirements is available from any state department of education, superintendent of schools, or a certification advisory committee.

Besides the basic music courses, an elementary-school music teacher should also study the techniques of Orff, Suzuki, Kodaly, and Dalcroze. He or she must have patience, enjoy working and communicating with children, be creative, and have good leadership qualities. Piano, guitar, and singing skills are very important for an elementary schoolteacher. According to the National Education Association, the average yearly salary for public elementary schoolteachers in 1988/89 was $28,909, with higher salaries in the Northeast and the West.

Secondary School Teaching

Secondary schoolteachers, like elementary schoolteachers, must have a bachelor's degree and must be certified by the state. About 1.2 million secondary or high school teachers were employed in 1988. According to the National Education Association, the average secondary public schoolteacher's salary in 1988/89 was $30,300 yearly, with higher salaries in the Northeast and

West. Approximately 4.8 percent of secondary schoolteachers are music teachers.

In a secondary school, the music program depends upon the size of the school budget. In a small school, one or two instructors may have the responsibility for all the music programs. In a large school, several music teachers may be on staff, each with a specialty. Where a school has a large enrollment, it is possible to have a band, an orchestra, and a choir.

School music teachers must be qualified to teach (and coach) voice and instruments, as well as conduct and direct the band, orchestra, and choir. Music appreciation, music history, theory, and ensemble work are also taught in the secondary schools.

Besides the basic courses, a music teacher must be prepared to direct a school musical play, prepare the band for the school's sporting events, and plan the music for school dances. A high school teacher must enjoy working with teenagers, have patience and an understanding of their nature, and have a good personality and good leadership qualities.

Teachers often work on community projects and work part time in nightclubs, resorts, club dates, private teaching, church music, or in music therapy programs.

College/University Teaching

According to the National Center for Education Statistics, in 1988 about 846,000 people were employed to teach various subjects in the nation's 3,587 colleges and universities. Approximately one-third of them were employed on a part-time basis.

College and university teachers are classified as professors, associate professors, assistant professors, and instructors. Instructors must have at least a master's degree, but because of the competition, a doctorate degree is more often required to get an appointment. Some states require several years of experience teaching public school before granting a college or university position.

Student enrollment in the 1990s is expected to remain steady, and employment opportunities will be based on turnover. In 1987/88, 6,703 students graduated with a bachelor's degree in music; 3,192 with a master's; and 502 with a doctorate.

A 1988 survey by the National Center for Education Statistics shows an average salary for professors to be $50,420; for associate professor, $37,530; assistant professor, $31,160; and instructor, $23,660 (for a nine-month contract).

In colleges, universities, and conservatories, the music teacher is a specialist and is hired as such. He or she teaches a specific instrument or specializes in harmony and theory, composition, conducting, voice, or another music or music related course.

The Chronicle of Higher Education (1255 Twenty-Third Street, N.W., Washington, DC 20037) has a want-ad section that advertises openings in colleges and universities for teachers, administrators, and directors.

Where to Get Training and Information

There are 640 colleges and universities that offer music education. The National Association of Schools of Music (NASM, 11250 Roger Bacon Drive, Suite 21, Reston, VA 22090) has a directory available that lists accredited institutions and major degree programs.

For information on college and university teaching, write to the following organizations:

National Council for Accreditation of Teacher Education (NCATE)
2029 K Street, N.W.
Suite 500
Washington, DC 20005

American Association of University Professors
1012 14th Street, N.W.
Washington, DC 20005

Information about teachers' unions can be obtained by writing to the following address:

American Federation of Teachers
555 New Jersey Avenue, N.W.
Washington, DC 20001

For general teaching information, contact the NEA:

National Education Association
1201 16th Street, N.W.
Washington, DC 20036

The following organizations have information, publications, seminars, conventions, and music educator members:

American Music Conference
303 East Wacker Drive
Suite 1214
Chicago, IL 60601

American Council on Education
One Dupont Circle
Washington, DC 20036

American Orff-Schulwerk Association
P.O. Box 391089
Cleveland, OH 44139-5366

College Music Society
202 West Spruce Street
Missoula, MT 59802

Music Educators National Conference (MENC)
1902 Association Drive
Reston, VA 22091

Music Teachers National Association
617 Vine Street
Suite 1432
Cincinnati, OH 45202-1420

National Association of Schools of Music
11250 Roger Beacon Drive
Suite 21
Reston, VA 22090

Organization of American Kodaly Educators
Music Department
Nicholls State University
Thibodaux, LA 70310

Suzuki Association of the Americas
P.O. Box 354
Muscatine, IA 52761

American Musicological Society
201 South 34th Street
Philadelphia, PA 19104

National School Orchestra Association
345 Maxwell Drive
Pittsburgh, PA 15236-2067

Private Instruction

Teaching privately can be a wonderful way of earning a living. It can be done in your own home, in the student's home, or in a studio. Some private teachers rent studio space from a local music shop or work at a small music school. You can teach full, or part time, depending, of course, on economics, population, and competition in your area.

A very important side effect of teaching is that you constantly polish your own talents by keeping in touch with your roots. It's also a good way to become known among your peers. The most gratifying reward from teaching is watching your students learn and grow from your willingness to share your knowledge and experience. The most popular instruments presently are the piano, the accordion, the guitar, and voice.

If the local schools are large enough to have a good music program, you'll find many children wanting to learn band instruments as well. Trumpet, clarinet, saxophone, flute, violin, and drums are very popular instruments. Your teaching schedule will probably start around three in the afternoon, when the school day ends.

Fees for private teaching range from $15 to $60 per hour, depending on your geographical location, instrument, status in the business, and the market.

If you find a large number of people interested in studying one instrument, you might explore the possibility of group classes. A studio that also carries instruments, accessories, and sheet music, and does instrument repairs, can be a good business in the right location.

Local music shops sometimes advertise for teachers in the local newspapers help-wanted columns. A teacher wanting to start a private practice can send out flyers; advertise in a trade paper, local newspaper; school, church, or community bulletin board; and hang up a shingle.

Here is a list of organizations that dispense information and publications related to private teaching:

The National Guild of Piano Teachers
P.O. Box 1807
Austin, TX 78767-1807

Keyboard Teachers Association International Inc.
361 Pin Oak Lane
Westbury, NY 11590

American Accordion Association
P.O. Box 616
Mineola, NY 11501
National Association of Teachers of Singing
2800 University Boulevard, N.
Jacksonville, FL 32211
New York Singing Teachers Association
884 West End Avenue
New York, NY 10025

The Superintendent of Documents has a booklet entitled "Starting and Managing a Business from Your Home." For a free catalog send a self-addressed, stamped envelope to the Consumer Information Center, P.O. Box 100, Pueblo, CO 81002.

Adult Education

Evening adult education centers offer courses in everything from sewing to socializing, including music; writing it, performing it, and appreciating it. There are classes in piano, guitar, singing, songwriting, opera, and musical theater. A teacher who can create an interesting program might be able to attract enough students to fill a classroom and supplement her or his income.

Training Aids

Another area open to teachers is the development of teaching materials. Educational materials—such as handbooks on teaching and music, and audio and video training programs—have to be developed and produced. Workshops, lectures, and clinics on music are all possible sources of employment. Possible topics include demonstrations of musical instruments, or lectures on music history, new techniques, or career opportunities.

BAND DIRECTOR

The band director is a conductor and the person responsible for musical extravaganzas at football games. There are about as many band directors as there are colleges, universities, and high schools. Some of the larger universities employ two, three, or even four band directors. The College Band Directors National Association (University of Texas, P.O. Box 8028, University Station, Austin, TX 78713-8028) has approximately 1,050 members and estimates that there are about 2,000 college band directors.

Although a band director is primarily a conductor, he or she is required to have a degree in music education. Since a degree in music education does not concentrate on preparing someone for conducting, it is up to the individual to be self-motivated and take additional courses in performance and conducting. Most large universities with a good band program can prepare someone for a career in band directing.

The difference between a band director and an orchestra conductor is the instrumentation and the repertoire. A band is made up of brass, woodwinds, and percussion, and the repertoire is more contemporary, and generally in a march tempo. Band directors work with students, teaching them music as the students learn to play their instruments.

Band directors usually start at the high school level and work their way up to a university position after gaining the necessary experience. Depending on the size of the school, their responsibilities may include producing whole shows, from creating the concept to writing the arrangements, from designing the marching routines to staging the band's performance.

Salaries are commensurate with those of teachers, but in a larger school situation where there are extra shows and concerts, a band director has the opportunity to earn extra money. Guest conducting, clinics, workshops, lectures, and private teaching can also add to a band director's income.

There are better job opportunities in a high growth area, but there are sometimes up to 50 applicants for one job opening. *The Chronicle of Higher Education* (1255 Twenty-Third Street, N.W., Washington, DC 20037) has a want-ad section that sometimes lists openings for band directors.

MUSIC LIBRARIAN

A music librarian must love music and enjoy working with records, music books, and scores. Music librarians work in public libraries, conservatories, college/university libraries, the Library of Congress, symphony orchestras, opera companies, licensing agencies, publishing companies, radio and television stations, music preparation houses, and sheet music retailers. Necessary skills include being able to read a score, music copying, microfilming, cataloging, operating a computer, binding, typing, restoring, filing, and even speaking a foreign language. A good knowledge of the recordings and repertoire of classical, ethnic, jazz, and popular music is necessary.

Most public and academic libraries require a master's degree in library science (MLS), preferably from an American Library Association accredited school, along with a master's degree in music (MM). There are 59 universities and colleges that offer an accredited MLS. A list of schools is available from the American Library Association. Send a self-addressed stamped envelope to Accredited List, American Library Association/COA, 50 East Huron Street, Chicago, IL 60611.

Working as a librarian for a symphony orchestra or opera company requires the ability to read a score, copy off parts and add notations, coordinate the purchase or rental of compositions for upcoming performances, and distribute and collect the parts for the rehearsals and the performances. In smaller orchestras, this job is usually done by one of the musicians.

A music librarian at a radio station is responsible for cataloging and filing all the records and tapes. He or she is sometimes referred to as the music director and works with the program director in selecting music for the various shows.

Working conditions for music librarians are pleasant, but the job market is tight. Openings depend on turnover. Salaries range from $15,000 to $30,000 per year in a college, university, or conservatory; $1,300 to $30,000 in a public library; $23,000 in an orchestra; and $14,000 to $27,000 at a radio or TV station.

The Music Library Association maintains a placement service along with a publication that keeps its members informed. There are approximately two thousand members in MLA, and an additional thousand subscribers to their publication. For more information write to The Music Library Association, P.O. Box 487, Canton, MA 02021.

MUSIC CRITIC

A music critic is a musician first and a reporter second. He or she must love music and writing about it. A critic must have a good ear, a well-rounded knowledge of all music styles, both old and new, and a familiarity with the standard repertoire. The ability to play an instrument, read music, and follow a score is essential for good criticism. A knowledge of the history and background of the style of music being reviewed is also important. A critic must have good writing skills and be able to express in words what he or she has heard in sound.

Critics work for newspapers and magazines and should be able to write in a style that is entertaining, stimulating, informative, and understandable to readers. A critic must know the audience for whom he or she is writing.

Presently there are three schools that offer courses in music criticism; however, workshops and seminars are sponsored by the Music Critics Association (7 Pine Court, Westfield, NJ 07090). The association has 240 members and holds an annual meeting, usually at a major musical event.

Becoming a music critic takes self-motivation and on-the-job training. Someone wanting to become a music critic could write free articles for a college newspaper or a small community paper. After gaining some experience and credits, he or she could try to get work as a free-lance writer or as a stringer (free-lance reporter). Eventually these assignments might lead to a job as an assistant critic. The job market is very tight. Many college and university music teachers work part time as stringers to supplement their incomes.

Since a music critic is a reporter, the salaries are negotiated by the American Newspaper Guild, and according to the Bureau of Labor Statistics, in 1989 the salary range for reporters was about $250 to $785 a week, with the majority earning $500 a week.

RELIGIOUS MUSIC

Religious music offers opportunities for music directors, organists, choir directors, and singers. Some jobs are full time, and some are part time. In order to have a career in religious music, you must enjoy playing the organ and working with a choir. But, most importantly, you must have a good feel for and understanding of religious music. Salaries range from $3,500 to $25,000 part time, and $15,000 to $50,000 full time.

Catholic Service

Before the early 1960s, the only music played in the Catholic church was traditional, with the mass delivered in Latin. However, the mass is now in English, and contemporary music has been introduced into the Catholic church. Folk, rock, and jazz masses have become commonplace.

Training

Choosing a college or university that specializes in organ and church music is very important. That can be discussed with your clergy or your teacher. It would be a good idea to combine your music education with business, as well as other performing arts courses.

The NASM directory lists accredited colleges and universities along with their degree programs. Schools that offer instruction in religious music can be found in this directory. It is available from the National Association of Schools of Music, 11250 Roger Bacon Drive, No. 5, Reston, VA 22090.

There are many organizations that have seminars, workshops, and publications geared to inform and educate as well as maintain and improve the standards of organ, chorale, and church music.

Minister of Music

The minister (or director) of music handles the responsibilities of all the music, and may have a choirmaster and an organist under her or his supervision. Besides the duties of supervising the music, a director may have to work with community projects, youth and senior citizen projects, and business administration. In some congregations, the music director is also the organist and the choir director.

The minister of music must have a background in church liturgy, harmony and theory, Gregorian chant, keyboard, choir, conducting, composition, hymns and traditional music as well as contemporary music styles. He or she also needs some business administrative abilities and a well-rounded knowledge of the arts.

There is no substitute for experience, and working with a music director, singing in the choir, and assisting the organist can provide valuable on-the-job training. In order to be a church organist, you must be able to read music, accompany singers and choirs, and perform as a soloist. Besides technique and a thorough knowledge of harmony and theory, the organist must also be familiar with the liturgical hymns and the repertoire from Gregorian chant to contemporary. The ability to improvise is also an asset.

A church organist sometimes free-lances from one congregation to another. For example, you may perform for a Catholic service one day, accompany a choir in a protestant church the next, then play for a Jewish service in a synagogue. The more knowledge you have of the needs of the different denominations, the more versatile you can be.

The organist is on call for weddings and funerals. This is an added source of income, and the fee is approximately $50 to $100 per service, depending on the congregation. Working outside the church can also supplement an income.

Choir Directors

A choir director must have a good knowledge of voice, vocal ranges, piano and organ, conducting, harmony and theory, arranging, Gregorian chant, hymns, liturgy, and the standard as well as the contemporary church repertoire. Besides the technical training, a choir director must have a good feel for religious music and a talent for blending voices.

Some congregations hire professional singers to work as soloists or to be part of the chorus. Some choruses are professional, and some are a mixture of professional singers and members of the congregation. Others are completely nonprofessionals; it all depends on the budget and the size of the congregation. An organist and a choir director must know how to handle both professional and nonprofessional singers.

Singers

A singer must have a good background in harmony and theory, Gregorian chant, liturgy, and hymns. Sight-singing skills are essential, since singers work in different denominations and are often introduced to new and different literature. A singer must also have the ability to sing in other languages, such as Latin, Italian, French, Spanish, Hebrew, German, and Greek.

Some wedding and funeral services use staff singers; however, outside vocalists are hired from time to time, depending on the situation. Fees range from $50 to $100. Singers also earn a living as voice teachers and vocal coaches or working in opera companies, musical theater, community projects, music therapy programs, club dates, nightclubs, or recording sessions.

Cantors

Cantors are singers that lead the Jewish service by chanting the prayers. Cantors work on a full-time or part-time basis, depending on the size of the congregation and the budget. Cantors also supplement their income by conducting the chorus and teaching Hebrew, Bible, and religion to the young, as well as preparing them for their Bar Mitzvah.

Study to become a cantor is done at the Cantorial Institute, which is part of the Jewish Theological Seminary, the Hebrew

Union College, or Yeshiva University, The course of study includes Hebrew, religion, the Bible, and history of Jewish music, in addition to sight-singing, harmony, theory, vocal repertoire, style, all the prayer chants, and cantillation of the Torah. Studying voice is usually done privately with a teacher outside the school.

Gospel Music

Gospel music is a big part of the music industry. Some record and publishing companies specialize only in gospel music, and record sales are in the millions. Live gospel concerts draw thousands of fans, while TV and radio audiences number in the millions. Gospel music comes in a variety of musical styles and employs many singers, instrumentalists, songwriters, composers, conductors, and arrangers.

Billboard and *Cashbox,* the music business weekly magazines, have feature sections on gospel music. News and business are discussed, along with a chart showing the record sales of gospel music. Buyers of gospel or sacred music make up 3 percent of the market.

ORGANIZATIONS AND PUBLICATIONS

Gospel Music Association
38 Music Square West
Nashville, TN 37203

The Hymn Society of America
Texas Christian University
P.O. Box 30854
Fort Worth, TX 76129

American Guild of Organists
475 Riverside Drive
Suite 1260
New York, NY 10115

National Forum for Greek Orthodox Church Musicians
1700 North Walnut
Suite 302
Bloomington, IN 47404

Church Music Association of America
Sacred Music (publication)
548 Lafond Avenue
St. Paul, MN 55103

Cantors Assembly
150 Fifth Avenue
New York, NY 10011

MUSIC THERAPY

If you've ever entertained in a prison, hospital, or a nursing home and you've witnessed your music bringing a smile to people's faces, then you've seen some of the therapeutic value of music. Music can get people to the center of the floor and dancing, or just put them in a romantic mood. Play a favorite song, and watch someone's mood change as you stir up an old memory.

Music goes beyond just entertainment. Coupled with the science and art of healing, it becomes a useful tool in diagnosing and treating mental and physical illnesses. Music therapy has existed since the beginning of civilization, and yet only recently has it become recognized as a valid method of treatment by the modern medical profession. The use of music therapy came into focus around 1950 and is still a new and growing field.

There are over 72 colleges and universities that have accredited programs in music therapy. Ten of those award master's degrees, and eight award master's degrees and doctorates. The course of study is music therapy, anthropology, sociology, psychology, music, and general studies. Training is completed under the supervision of a registered music therapist. There are approximately 175 approved training and internship facilities in the United States.

Music therapists work with physicians and psychiatrists in mental institutions, geriatric centers, day-care centers, clinics for physically handicapped children, civilian and veterans' hospitals, and correctional institutions. According to the National Association for Music Therapy (505 Eleventh Street, S.E., Washington, DC 20003), there are approximately 6,000 people working in the profession. Of these, 4,000 are members of the association, and of those, 3,800 are certified as music therapists. Salaries range from $14,000 to $45,000, and even with the economy and the budget cuts, the job market seems to be healthy.

A music therapist should know how to play the piano, the guitar, other stringed instruments, wind instruments (like the recorder), and percussion and rhythm instruments. A therapist must enjoy working with people and have a desire to help them. Besides good physical and mental health, a therapist must have imagination, stamina, and a good sense of humor.

A music therapist uses playing and teaching instruments; singing, composing, and writing songs; as well as playing records to bring about a change in a patient. The process may involve using soothing, dissonant, or ethnic music to stir up emotions and draw them out. Playing an instrument can restore the patient's coordination, and singing can help overcome speech and breathing problems. Using group music activities helps patients build confidence and become aware of themselves and the world around them. Observing, diagnosing, and treating with music can restore mental and physical health. A therapist works with small and large groups and sometimes on a one-to-one basis.

A directory of schools and training facilities is available from the National Association for Music Therapy. It includes a list of accredited colleges and universities. Volunteer and part-time help is needed in summer programs, drug and alcohol rehabilitation centers, hospitals, nursing homes, and mental institutions. Working in a summer music therapy program should give you a good idea of whether this is a career for you. Openings are sometimes advertised in the help-wanted section of the newspaper.

The American Association for Music Therapy (P.O. Box 27177, Philadelphia, PA 19118) is another organization that is made up of music therapists. They too have a directory of schools and training facilities.

MILITARY MUSIC

The five branches of the military that offer opportunities for musicians and singers are the army, the navy, the air force, the marines, and the coast guard. Together they represent approxi mately 102 bands stationed in and around the United States and all over the world. The army has two special bands stationed in the Washington, D.C. area: The U.S. Army Band, Pershing's Own, and the U.S. Army Field Band. The navy, the air force, and the marines each have one special band stationed in Washington. Their responsibilities range from parades and ceremonies to playing for dances at the White House.

The music requirements for a position in one of these special bands are very high, and auditions are arranged only when there is a vacancy. Also, a security clearance is necessary because the bands perform in and around the White House and come into close contact with the president. In fact, the marine corps band is called

The President's Own. There is also a special band at each military academy and one on Paris Island.

The music ranges from symphonic to march and ceremonial to dance. The bands vary in size from a large symphony orchestra of about 40 to 251 pieces to an eighteen-piece dance band to a small combo. Military performance groups are classified as symphony orchestra, concert band, stage band, field band, dance band, chorus, chorale, drum-and-bugle corps, drum-and-fife corps, string ensemble, soloists, jazz-rock-country-blues combos, and special entertainment groups. The air force has a famous chorus known as The Singing Sergeants.

There are approximately 50 army bands, 17 navy bands, 14 marine bands, 20 air force bands, and one coast guard band. They are classified as premier, special, and field.

Before you consider the military, you must understand that the military book of rules comes first. There is a certain code of dress, grooming, and discipline that you must be able to adjust to. Also, there is the term of enlistment, depending on the branch of service. It can be from a minimum of three to four years to as long as you want. If you choose, it can be your whole career.

If you are not assigned to one of the special bands, it could mean being stationed far away from your home, even overseas. Some of the special bands and choruses go on tours as representatives of the United States Armed Forces and entertain all over the world. If you like to travel, that could be a positive aspect of music in the military.

The military needs men and women instrumentalists, singers, composers, arrangers and orchestrators, copyists, conductors, music directors, librarians, accompanists, teachers, and instrument repair technicians. An applicant must have a musical specialty, a background in harmony and theory, the ability to read music, and the ability to meet the standard enlistment requirements before auditioning. An audition can be set up through your local recruiter, or directly with the commander of a special band. Depending on the applicant's qualifications, the audition may be in Washington, D.C., or at a local installation.

Upon completion of basic training, which can be from 8 to 12 weeks, depending on the branch of the service, the musician is then sent to the military school of music in Norfolk, Virginia, for six months. After completing the course of study, he or she is then assigned to a band. If qualified, he or she can also choose to continue studying advanced courses in conducting, composing, and arranging. The training facility is on the same level as a civilian conservatory, and it is recognized and accredited as such. The government will also pay tuition costs for those who wish to continue studying on their own time at a local college or university.

The starting grade is E-3, which is higher than the regular recruits, and the salary and working conditions are comparable to civilian occupations. Starting salaries range from $16,000 to $24,000 a year. Benefits include a thirty-day vacation, full medical care, commissary and post exchange privileges, as well as pension and retirement benefits.

There is a need for good musicians and singers in the military, especially woodwind and horn players. With the incentives that are being offered, it might be worth your while to examine the possibilities. Your local recruiter should have a video and information showing the opportunities available for musicians in that particular branch of the service. Openings for instrumentalists and vocalists are advertised in the *International Musicians' Journal*. In rare cases, an assignment with a special band does not require basic training nor attending the military school of music.

For information see your local recruiter or write to the following addresses:

Commandant of the Marine Corps
Field Military Music Section (MPC-60)
Headquarters U. S. Marine Corps
Washington, DC 20380-0001

Head, Music Branch
Naval Military Personnel Command
(NMPC-654)
Washington, DC 20370-9990

Department of the Air Force
Chief, Air Force Bands and Music Branch (SAF/PAGB)
Room 4A120
Office of Public Affairs
Washington, DC 20330-1000

Recruiting
U.S. Coast Guard Band
U.S. Coast Guard Academy
New London, CT 06320-4195

Sergeant Major, Army Bands
Att: ATZI-AB
Alexandria, VA 22332-1320

CHAPTER 9

MORE MUSIC BUSINESS

AGENTS

Booking agencies come in various sizes, from a local one-agent operation to the large national firms that maintain offices in many cities, a large staff of agents, and departments that cover all the categories in show business. An agent generally receives a commission of 10 percent or 15 percent, depending upon the situation.

It takes an agent more time and energy to book a $100 act than it does to book a $10,000 act, and since most agents already have a roster of artists and a circuit of clubs they book, it's not easy for them to take a chance on an unknown. Usually, in the beginning stages of a performing career, an artist has to act as his or her own agent and manager—knocking on doors, showcasing, sending out publicity, working small clubs.

It takes time to build a reputation in order for an agent to have the confidence to book an act. As artists become more popular, they begin to get recognition from local agents, and then, through the same self-motivation and persistence, they will get the larger agencies to notice them.

The local yellow pages list agents under Theatrical Agents, Musicians, and Orchestras and Bands. Some agents advertise in the *International Musician.* Many agents are franchised in more than one of the unions: AFM, AFTRA, SAG, Actors' Equity, AGMA, or AGVA. Each of these unions maintains an agency list. The trade papers *(Variety, Backstage, Showbusiness, Cashbox, Billboard, The Hollywood Reporter, Daily Variety,* and *Pollstar)* contain a lot of information about agents and bookings.

PERSONAL MANAGERS

A personal manager is the one who is responsible for all the planning and strategies involved with developing an artist's career. A personal manager is involved with contract negotiations, record companies, publicity, bookings, and even solving personal problems.

In the case of the artist who earns a lot of money, a business manager generally handles investments, accounting, and taxes. The artist and manager must have a good personal relationship and a mutual trust for each other since a manager generally has power of attorney. Some managers have a flat fee, and others have a sliding fee with a maximum cut-off point. Fees can range from 15 percent to 50 percent of the gross, and all expenses are usually paid by the artists.

Like the agent, a manager can't make money from an act that doesn't command large fees. However, unlike the agent, a manager who can recognize talent and an artist's potential will sometimes work at developing an unknown artist into a star.

Performers who go on a concert tour need a whole cast of support personnel to get that show on the road. That includes the road manager, stage manager, roadies, lighting and sound technicians, back-up musicians, and singers. All of these support personnel are learning their trade from the road up. This valuable on-the-job training can lead any of them into careers as concert promoters, personal managers, booking agents, producers, and even artists.

Organizations that have a membership of personal managers are the National Conference of Personal Managers (East and West), 1650 Broadway, Suite 705, New York, NY 10019, and the Nashville Association of Talent Directors. Billboard's 1990 *International Talent and Touring Directory* lists approximately 3,600 booking agents, personal managers, public relations firms, and business management firms.

ARTS MANAGERS

Arts managers represent instrumentalists, vocalists, conductors, orchestras, ensembles, and dancers in the field of serious music. An arts manager in this field not only books the artist but also develops the artist's career. A manager is generally responsible for many details when coordinating a booking, such as promotion, transportation, advertising, ticket sales, and accommodations. For information, write:

The Association of Performing Artists Presenters
1112 16th Street, N.W.
Suite 620
Washington, DC 20036

ARTS ADMINISTRATORS

Arts administrators manage and run symphony orchestras, opera companies, and community arts projects. The general manager is responsible for the entire staff, which includes fund-raising, public relations, program planning, library, and ticket sales. Many musicians have found careers in management and administration preferable to a career in performing.

Many schools have courses and degree programs for performing arts management. Some subjects taught in such schools are concert promotion, talent booking and management, market research, administration of performing arts organizations, labor relations, public relations, grant proposal writing, and government and community resources.

TUNER/TECHNICIANS

It is estimated that there are over ten million pianos in this country—nine million in private homes and one million in schools and entertainment facilities. According to the Bureau of Labor Statistics, in 1989, approximately 7,500 people worked as piano tuners and technicians. Approximately two-thirds of all tuners are self-employed. The rest work for school systems, music stores, and piano manufacturers.

To tune a piano, the pitch of the 'A' string (440 pitch) is adjusted by turning the pin with a tuning hammer (which is really a wrench) until it matches the pitch of the tuning fork. All the other strings are adjusted in relation to the 'A' string. The tuner's ear is trained to listen for the interfering sound waves, or beats, as he or she pulls each string into pitch.

The hammers wear out from constant use, so the tuner files them smooth again. After filing, the hammers have to be voiced and the action regulated to take up the slack.

The tuner/technician carries special tools for repairing and replacing worn or broken parts and strings. Since the majority of work is done in private homes, the working conditions are pleasant; however, a tuner/technician must have a good personality and a good appearance in order to deal with the public successfully. It takes approximately 1 1/2 to 2 hours to tune a piano.

Although there are a lot of pianos in homes, it doesn't represent that much work. Most people tend to neglect regular maintenance, especially in bad economic times, and some avoid it completely. In hotels, schools, opera companies, and clubs, the pianos are usually tuned once a week.

Most tuners get their training on the job, by working under the guidance of an accomplished tuner/technician. It takes about four or five years to become a tuner. There are some schools that offer courses in tuning and maintenance. A partial list is available from the Piano Technicians Guild. There are also special schools for the blind and visually handicapped.

A list and evaluation of piano tuning correspondence schools is in the November 1990 issue of *Keyboard Magazine*. Back issues are available from Keyboard Back Issues, P.O. Box T, Gilroy, CA 95020.

A self-employed tuner can charge from $35 to $65 a tuning. Some technicians who are also good at woodworking specialize in rebuilding and refinishing pianos, and the profits from that add to their incomes. There is also a need for technicians to tune and repair electronic and pipe organs in churches, synagogues, auditoriums, theaters, schools, and private homes. And, with today's new technology, technicians are also needed to repair synthesizers, samplers, electric pianos, and amplifiers. A musician with a knowledge of electronics, who can also handle a soldering iron, should examine the possibilities of working in electronic instrument repair. For more information, write:

Piano Technicians Guild
4510 Belleview
Suite 100
Kansas City, MO 64111

MANUFACTURER-WHOLESALER-
RETAILER OF INSTRUMENTS

There are many opportunities for musicians in this area of the business—musicians who are willing to combine their talents with other skills such as marketing, sales, repairing, designing, and handcrafting. Every instrument and accessory has to be invented and designed.

Not only new instruments, but the standard instruments need improvements, new materials, and techniques. That calls for research and development engineers. And who would know better than a musician what sounds, feels, and plays better on her or his instrument? The ability to play several instruments is a big asset to an inventor.

A musician who has been influenced by the age of electronics and whose curiosity has led to the understanding of computers, chips, and circuitry, is standing on the threshold of electronic instruments—the invention and design, and also the building, testing, repairing, demonstration, selling, and performing of these instruments.

A musician who is good at woodworking and finishing can turn to building guitars, violins, cellos, pianos, and other stringed instruments. Musicians who enjoy working with metal, soldering, shaping, plating, and machining can also find careers in building brass instruments.

Every instrument built needs to be inspected and tested, and that takes someone with a thorough knowledge of the instrument, and music. Many instrument manufacturers have training programs so that a musician can gain experience on the job. In some cases, after gaining experience, a musician can also build instruments in her or his own shop. Other opportunities in manufacturing are management, sales, product development, promotion, advertising, and demonstrating.

A musician who can diagnose and repair instruments is always in demand. Musical instrument technology courses at colleges and universities can prepare someone for a career in woodwind, brass, string, and percussion repair. A repair person can also own and operate her or his own repair shop. The shop could include instrument and sheet music sales, as well as private instruction.

The *Purchaser's Guide To The Music Industries* is a journal that has information on manufacturers of musical instruments, industry associations, industry schools, the Canadian music industry, keyboard manufacturers, and much more. For information write:

The Music Trades
80 West Street
P.O. Box 432
Englewood, NJ 07631

National Association of Band Instrument Manufacturers
(NABIM)
136 West 21st Street
New York, NY 10011–3212

National Association of Professional
　Band Instrument Repair Technicians (NAPBIRT)
P.O. Box 51
Normal, IL 61761

The National Association of Music Merchants promotes the study and growth of music markets; the enhancement of equitable and constructive legislation; training for members and their employees; developing technicians for the servicing of music products; researching, gathering, and organizing industry statistics; and conducting trade shows, educational exhibits, and national meetings for all its members. NAMM also maintains a management and sales training institute. For more information:

National Association of Music Merchants (NAMM)
  5140 Avenida Encinas
  Carlsbad, CA 92008–4391
  1-800-767-6266

BIBLIOGRAPHY

BROCHURE

Careers in Music, Music Educators National Conference, 1902 Association Drive, Reston, VA 22091.

Careers with Music, Incorporated Society of Musicians, 10 Stratford Place, London, Ontario, Canada W1N9AE.

BOOKS

Careers in Music

Exploring Careers in Music, American Music Conference, 303 Wacker Drive, Suite 1214, Chicago, IL 60601; or from Music Educators National Conference, 1902 Association Drive, Reston, VA 22901, 1990.

The Music/Record Career Handbook, Joseph Csida, Billboard Publications, New York, 1980.

Opportunities in Acting, Dick Moore, VGM Career Horizons, Lincolnwood, IL, 1985.

Opportunities in Broadcasting, Elmo I. Ellis, VGM Career Horizons, Lincolnwood, IL, 1986.

Music Business

The Music Business, Dick Weissman, Crown Publishers, Inc., New York, 1979.
Music Business Handbook, David Baskerville, Ph.D., The Sherwood Company, Denver, CO, 1985.
This Business of Music, Sidney Shemel and William Krasilovsky, Billboard Publications, New York, 1985.
More About This Business of Music, Sidney Shemel and William Krasilovsky, Billboard Publications, New York, 1989.
Encyclopedia of the Music Business, Harvey Rachlin, Harper and Row, New York, 1981.
Inside the Music Publishing Industry, Paula Dranov, Knowledge Industries Publications Inc., White Plains, NY, 1980.
The Platinum Rainbow, Bob Monaco and James Riordan, Swordsman Press, Sherman Oaks, CA, 1980.
Successful Artist Management, Frascogna and Hetherington, Watson-Guptill Publications, New York, 1978.
Promoting Rock Concerts, Stein and Zalkind, Schirmer Books, Division of Macmillan Publishing Co., Inc., New York, NY, 1979.
Music Business Directory (vols. 1 & 2), Robert Allen Livingston, La Costa Music Business Consultants, P.O. Box 147, Cardiff, CA 92007, 1991.
Principles of Orchestra Management, American Symphony Orchestra League, 777 Fourteenth Street, N.W., Suite 500, Washington, DC 20005.

Books on Getting Started

Through the Jingle Jungle, Steve Karmen, Billboard Books, New York, 1989.
How to Make Money in Music, Herby Harris and Lucien Farrar, Arco Publishing Company, Inc., New York, NY, 1978.
Making Money, Making Music, James Dearing, Writers Digest Books, Cincinnati, OH 1982.
Breaking Into the Music Business, Alan H. Siegal, Cherry Lane Books, Port Chester, NY, 1983.
Making It with Music, Kenny Rogers, Harper and Row Publishers, New York, NY 1978.
Pianist Progress, Helen Dress Ruttencutter, Thomas V. Crowell Publishers, New York, NY, 1979.
Musicians Guide to the Road, Gary Burton, Watsin Guptill Publishing, Division of Billboard, New York, NY 1981.

Starting Your Own Band, Rock, Disco, Folk, Jazz, C&W, Lani Van Ryzin, Walker & Company, New York, NY, 1980.

Starting Your Own Rock Band, Cynthia Dagnal, Contemporary Books, Chicago, IL, 1983.

Composing and Conducting

Scoring for Films, Earl Hagen, Alfred Publishing Company, Inc., Los Angeles, CA, 1971.

The Schillinger System of Musical Composition (2 volumes), Joseph Schillinger, Da Capo, New York, NY, 1978.

Principles of Orchestration, Nikolay Rimsky-Korakov, Dover Publications, New York, NY, 1964.

Twentieth Century Harmony, Vincent Persichetti, W. W. Norton & Co., Inc., New York, NY 1961.

On the Track, Fred Karlin and Rayburn Wright, Schirmer Books, A Division of Macmillan, Inc., New York, NY, 1990.

Orchestration, Cecil Forsyth, Dover Press, New York, NY, 1982.

The Technique of Orchestration, Kent Wheeler Kennan, Prentice-Hall, Inc., Englewood Cliffs, NJ, 1970.

Underscore, Frank Skinner, Criterian Music Corp., New York, NY, 1960.

The Contemporary Arranger, Don Sebesky, Alfred Publishing Co., Sherman Oaks, CA, 1975.

Sounds and Score, Henry Mancini, Cherry Lane Music Co. Inc., Greenwich, CT 1973.

Handbook of Conducting, Herman Scherchen, Da Capo Press, New York, NY, 1978.

Choral Conducting, Archibald T. Davison, Harvard University Press, Cambridge, MA, 1940.

A Music Notation Primer, Glen R. Rosecrans, Pen Pusher Publications, Woodland Hills, CA, 1976.

The Nashville Numbers System, Arthur D. Levine, Gibraltar Press Publications, Nashville, TN, 1981.

Songwriting and Copyright

Songwriters Market, Writers Digest Books, Cincinnati, OH 45207.

Songwriters Rhyming Dictionary, Jane Shaw Whitfield, Wilshire Book Company, North Hollywood, CA, 1975.

Songwriters Rhyming Dictionary, Sammy Cahn, Facts on File, New York, NY, 1983.

Great Songs of Madison Avenue, Peter and Craig Norback, Times Books, New York, NY, 1976.

Musicians Guide to Copyright, U. Gunner Erickson and Edward R. Hearn, Charles Scribner and Sons, New York, NY, 1983.

Songwriters Success Manual, Lee Pincus, Music Press, New York, NY, 1976.

The Songwriters Handbook, Harvey Rachlin, Funk & Wagnalls, New York, NY, 1977.

The Songwriters Handbook, Tom T. Hall, Nashville, TN, 1987.

The Songwriters Guide to Collaboration, Walter Carter, Cincinnati, OH, 1988.

How to Turn Your Songs into Gold, vols. 1 & 2 (audio-book), Norman Weiser, Halsey International, 24 Music Square West, Nashville, TN, 37203, 1990.

Recording

Modern Recording Techniques, Robert E. Runstein, Howard W. Sams & Co., Indianapolis, IN, 1986.

The Record Producers Handbook, Don Gere, Acrobat Books, Los Angeles, CA, 1978.

How to Make and Sell Your Own Record, Diane Sward Rapaport, Putnam Publications Group, New York, 1988.

Musicians Guide to Independent Record Production, Will Connelly, Contemporary Books, Chicago, IL, 1981.

The Record Producers, Tobler and Grundy, State Mutual Books, New York, NY, 1982.

Introduction to Professional Recording Techniques, Bruce Bartlett, Howard W. Sams & Co., Indianapolis, IN, 1987.

Audio in Media, Stanley R. Alten, Wadsworth Publishing Co., Belmont, CA, 1986.

The MIDI Home Studio, Howard Massey, Amsco Publications, New York, NY, 1988.

Multi Track Recording, Dominic Milano, H. Leonard Books, Milwaukee, WI, 1988.

TRADE PAPERS, JOURNALS, AND MAGAZINES

Billboard, 1515 Broadway, New York, NY 10036.

Cashbox, 157 West 57th Street, Suite 1402, New York, NY 10019.

The Hollywood Reporter, 6715 Sunset Boulevard, Hollywood, CA 90028.

Variety, 475 Park Avenue South, New York, NY 10016.

Daily Variety, 5700 Wilshire Boulevard, Los Angeles, CA 90036.

Backstage, 330 West 42nd Street, New York, NY 10036.

Showbusiness, 1501 Broadway, New York, NY 10036.

Downbeat, Maher Publications, 180 W. Park Avenue, Elmhurst, IL 60129.

Musician, P.O. Box 1923, Marion, OH 43305.

Keyboard, GPI Publications, 20085 Stevens Creek, Cupertino, CA, 95014-9967.

Modern Drummer, P.O. Box 480, Mount Morris, IL 61054-0480.

Guitar Player, GPI Publications, 20085 Stevens Creek, Cupertino, CA 95014-9967.

Guitar World, Harris Publications, 1115 Broadway, New York, NY 10010.

Guitar International, Cherry Lane Music Co., Inc., 110 Midland Avenue, Port Chester, NY 10573.

Frets, GPI Publications, 20085 Stevens Creek, Cupertino, CA 95014-9967.

International Musician, American Federation of Musicians, 1501 Broadway, New York, NY 10036.

Mix Magazine, 6400 Hollis Street, Suite 12, Emeryville, CA 94608, 1-800-233-9604.

Electronic Musician, 6400 Hollis Street, Suite 12, Emeryville, CA 94608, 1-800-233-9604.

Opera News, 1865 Broadway, New York, NY 10023.

Symphony Magazine, American Symphony Orchestra League, 777 14th Street, N.W., Washington, DC 20005.

High Fidelity/Musical America, 825 Seventh Avenue, New York, NY 10019.

DIRECTORIES

International Buyers Guide

International Talent and Touring Directory

Country Music Source Book

International Recording Equipment and Studio Directory

International Directory of Manufacturing & Packaging

Auditorium/Arena/Stadium Directory, Billboard Publications, 1515 Broadway, New York, NY 10036.

Musical America International Directory of Performing Arts, 825 Seventh Avenue, New York, NY 10019.

Music Industry Directory, Marquis Professional Publications, 200 East Ohio Street, Chicago, IL 60611, 1983.

Madison Avenue Handbook, Peter Glenn Publications, 17 East 48th Street, New York, NY 10017.

The Professional Singers Guide to New York, Richard Owens, AIMS, 3500 Maple Avenue, Suite 120, LB22 Dallas, TX 75219-3901.

National Association of Schools of Music (Directory and Handbook) 11250 Roger Bacon Drive, No. 5, Reston, VA 22090.

Suber's Guide to MEI Schools (Music & Entertainment Industry Schools), Charles Suber & Associates, Inc., 600 Dearborn Street, Chicago, IL.

Sterns Performing Arts Directory, 33 West 60th Street, New York, NY 10023.

Backstage Film TV & Tape Production Directory, Backstage Publications, 330 West 42nd Street, New York, NY 10036.

Backstage Handbook for Performing Artists, Sherry Eaker, Backstage Publications, 330 West 42nd Street, New York, NY 10036.

Broadcasting Yearbook, 1705 DeSales Street, N.W., Washington, DC 20036-4480.